3 4028 07800 0230
HARRIS COUNTY PUBLIC LIBRARY

641.57
Scri
Camp   W9-ASI-509
Feather guide : eating
well in the wild
$19.95
ocn123892295
1st ed.   09/13/2011

CAMP

THE BLACK

COOKING

FEATHER GUIDE

Eating Well in the Wild

BY MARK SCRIVER, WENDY GRATER, JOANNA BAKER

Published by

 THE **HELICONIA PRESS**
www.helipress.com

1576 Beachburg Road
Beachburg, Ontario K0J 1C0
www.helipress.com

Copyright © 2007 The Heliconia Press

All rights reserved. No part of this book may be reproduced in any form, or by any electronic, mechanical, digital, or other means, without permission in writing from the publisher.

Printed in Canada

First Edition

Written by: Mark Scriver, Wendy Grater, Joanna Baker
Edited by: Rebecca Sandiford, Debbie Higgins, Tim Shuff
Design and Layout: THUMPmedia

Library and Archives Canada Cataloguing in Publication

Scriver, Mark

   Camp cooking : the Black Feather guide : eating well in the wild / Mark Scriver, Wendy Grater, Joanna Baker ; editor, Rebecca Sandiford.

ISBN 978-1-896980-31-7

   1. Outdoor cookery. I. Sandiford, Rebecca, 1973- II. Grater, Wendy, 1954- III. Baker, Joanna, 1975- IV. Title.

TX823.S47 2007   641.5'782   C2007-902706-7

CAMP
THE BLACK
COOKING
FEATHER GUIDE

Eating Well in the Wild

Content

the nicest chapter campfire
been at late to bed the
Northern lights later th

Day 9
Up at 8:30 off at 10:30
from South. A little w
few swifts Scribes kills
one way water fight. A
developing behind us.
above Porcupine rapids on a pie
A few sprinkles as w
Than Porcupine river ea
if back ferrying below
in torrential downpour
swampy size Blew
passed a 3, Indians

ohe
breeze
the
iron
Marsh
station
beside it,
ted to
main
of
whatever
m
ream

INTRODUCTION

EATING WELL IN THE WILD

EATING WELL IN THE WILD Long ago, the Voyageurs paddled birch bark canoes across Canada's north in search of furs and trade. Traditionally, when a Voyageur returned home from his first trip beyond the Arctic Divide where all watersheds lead to the Arctic Ocean, he was awarded a *plume noire*, a black feather to wear proudly in his hat. Black Feather, the Wilderness Adventure Company, is a Canadian canoeing and wilderness travel outfitter. Since 1971, Black Feather has introduced thousands of paddlers and explorers to Canada's wilderness. Fostering many of the same values that the Voyageurs of yesteryear embodied (cooperation, skill development, environmental stewardship and adventure) Black Feather's guides and participants have collectively canoed, sea kayaked and hiked many thousands of miles. From the fabled Nahanni River to Ellesmere Island in the High Arctic, and from introductory weekend clinics for the novice to extended expeditions for the seasoned adventurer, Black Feather offers a wide variety of destinations and skill levels.

While Voyageurs typically sustained themselves with bland, monotonous and caloric food chosen largely because it would last, Black Feather has always aimed to provide meals that are delicious, varied and nutritious. Over the years, we have refined recipes, quantities and cooking methods based on experience and input from hundreds of guides and trip participants. We have tried new recipes, modified old ones and always been on the lookout for interesting food ideas. Sometimes our guides will bring back delicious ethnic recipes after an adventure abroad, or we'll learn tricks from the locals encountered on a trip. We aim to use as many whole, organic and fair-trade foods as possible to create well-balanced meals no matter what the group's dietary preferences or restrictions might be.

In addition to continually developing and perfecting our menus, Black Feather has also become a leader in advancing and improving outdoor equipment and methods of wilderness cooking and packing. The Black Feather barrel pack and harness, for example, were developed by Black Feather guides in the 1980's. Over the course of a decade, a series of barrel pack harness prototypes were used on Nahanni and Dumoine River trips, and each year the design was improved and modified based on experience. Barrel packs are now widely used in wilderness travel for the transport of food.

The Black Feather philosophy about food on the trail is that it should be one of the highlights of the day. In the camp kitchen, the great stories of the day are recounted, jokes are told, ideas are shared and the problems of the world are solved. There is always room in Black Feather's kitchen for someone to join in and help with the chopping of the onions, the shredding of the mozzarella or the stirring of the sauce. While we know we cannot feasibly be a five-star restaurant, we believe that each meal should be delicious and nutritious, presented with appeal and flair, and that the joy of sharing a wholesome and tasty meal, while watching the setting sun's golden rays work magic on the surrounding landscape, is what the experience is really all about.

Black Feather Camp Cooking: Eating Well in the Wild is the essential "how-to" guide to selecting and using equipment; planning meals and packing food for multi-day, multi-person trips; setting up a functional "kitchen" in the wilderness; and skillfully putting it all together to serve up some great meals. We've also detailed special considerations that are unique to preparing and optimizing meals for rafting/canoeing, sea kayaking and hiking trips, as well as included a sample menu to help you get started. Finally, you'll find a wide selection of some of our most delicious and reliable recipes that you can try for yourself.

Distilled from decades of experience, experimentation and good eating in the wilderness, *Black Feather Camp Cooking* was designed and written to help you successfully plan, pack and prepare everything you need to eat well in the wild. Enjoy.

Wendy Grater, Black Feather Director and Guide
Mark Scriver, Black Feather Senior Guide
Joanna Baker, Senior Guide

ABOUT THE AUTHORS

WENDY GRATER, *owner and director of Black Feather Wilderness Adventures, has been guiding and feeding people on camping trips for over 25 years. She's pioneered sea kayaking routes in Greenland, hiked remote Arctic wilderness and paddled almost every river Black Feather has run. Easygoing, yet committed to excellence, Wendy's energy and enthusiasm for sharing her love of the wild is contagious.*

MARK SCRIVER *is one of the most respected and accomplished paddlers in the world. He has taught whitewater canoeing, sea kayaking and other paddling and outdoor skills, and has been leading commercial trips for Black Feather since 1983. More recently, Mark authored 'Canoe Camping - An Essential Guide', co-authored 'Thrill of the Paddle' - an instructional whitewater canoeing book, and won the World Freestyle Canoeing Championships in 1997.*

JOANNA BAKER *has a passion for playing and cooking in the outdoors. Her quest for adventure has led her on many journeys, both professionally as a former instructor for the Canadian Outward Bound School and personally as an avid traveler. Not satisfied with the standard canoe trip menu, she strives to add a twist of creativity to her meal planning. Joanna contributed recipes, tips and tricks for this book in the hopes of inspiring others to get creative too!*

Wendy Grater

Mark Scriver

Joanna Baker

KITCHEN EQUIPMENT

CHAPTER 1

figure 1. "For health reasons, stainless steel or cast iron pots are preferred." *Camping specific pot sets are designed to pack together very efficiently.*

figure 2. "Furthermore, woks require less oil than a frying pan, and  if you run short of oil, you can add water as cooking progresses." *Woks are one of the most versatile pieces of cookware.*

figure 3. "... (a flat frying surface 9" x 20") is ideal for cooking pancakes ..." *A griddle is convenient, but only a viable option on trips for which space and weight aren't concerns.* figure 4. "... with a lid that will stay secured ..." *Pressure* cooker. figure 5. *Lexan utensils are* "lightweight and durable."

Most of the gear on our kitchen equipment list will be familiar and easily borrowed from your kitchen at home. We'll cover the basics and discuss some considerations, but remember that you can always substitute your preferences or use whatever is available.

POTS AND PANS

For health reasons, stainless steel or cast iron pots are preferred. Aluminum pots are less expensive but have been linked to Alzheimer's disease, and Teflon (especially if it is used at high temperatures) has been linked to cancer. Whether or not these scientific findings are completely conclusive, we prefer to err on the side of caution and use stainless steel whenever possible.

It is nice to have a large, 2 gallon (8 liter) pot for cooking or heating water, and then depending on the complexity of your menu and the size of your group, another three to five pots that nest inside each other, lids included.

If you cook over fire, the pots *will* get black, and it is a losing battle to try to avoid it. Keep the kitchen equipment in stuff sacks, and use pliers or leather gloves to handle them to prevent the spread of soot. The pots won't get sooty if you use cook stoves. You might consider having two pot sets, and if you go on a trip where you'll use stoves exclusively, take the set that never gets used on a fire. *(figure 1)*

WOKS

The wok is a very useful and versatile pot. It is ideal for frying vegetables and is big enough for a sauce, stir-fry or stew. It can also be used as a washing basin for dishes, and is perfect for making popcorn. Furthermore, woks require less oil than a frying pan, and if you run short of oil, you can add water as cooking progresses. For cooking over fire, woks with curved bottoms are better for scraping and serving, but if you're cooking on a stove, you will find flat-bottomed woks are more stable. *(figure 2)*

GRIDDLES AND FRYING PANS

For lightweight camping, many pot sets have lids that double as frying pans, but if you are not concerned with space or weight, a griddle (a flat frying surface 9" x 20") is ideal for cooking pancakes, bacon, or fish on an open fire or firebox. It can also function as a serving platter. If you trim your cutting board to the same size as the griddle, they will pack together neatly. If you're using stoves, griddles are less efficient, unless you're using a two-burner stove unit. Again, if you're not concerned with weight and a griddle is not suitable or available, you might consider bringing a proper frying pan that will produce better results than your double-duty pot lids. *(figure 3)*

PRESSURE COOKERS

The pressure cooker is a special pot with a lid that will stay secured as the pressure rises from heating the pot. It reduces cooking times by half and is particularly useful if conserving stove fuel is an issue, or at high altitudes where cooking times will be even further reduced. It is heavier, a bit bulkier and quite a bit more expensive than a regular pot, so it can be overkill for most camping situations. *(figure 4)*

UTENSILS AND DISHES

It's a good idea to keep the eating and kitchen utensils in a nylon apron with different pockets to keep them organized and easy to grab when you need them. Included among the kitchen utensils are a couple of large kitchen knives, one or two spatulas, a couple of large spoons for serving or mixing, a soup ladle, a whisk, a grater, a garlic press, a small strainer (for the dishwater), a can opener and channel-lock pliers that serve as a sturdy pot lifter.

There are lots of options for plates, bowls and cups, but this works: for each person, skip the bowl and use a deep plate made out of a polycarbonate thermoplastic (like Lexan), a good-sized insulated mug, and a stackable thermoplastic cup. The second cup can be used for soup or a second drink, or to measure ingredients while cooking. A couple of extra Lexan plates are useful to have around when you're chopping vegetables or grating cheese. You want to be careful not to scratch the Lexan plastic too much as this variety of plastic can be toxic if it leaches into your food. *(figure 5)*

A simple
coffee pot.

figure 6.

BOWLS One or two stainless steel mixing bowls are great for serving salad, mixing batter, or as a lid for the wok, and they'll pack easily with the wok.

COFFEE POT There are different options for making coffee but it's fun to make it in a tall 1 gallon (4 liter) pot with a handle so it can be swished or swung around to settle the grounds. Other options are to use a camping French-press coffee maker (like a Bodum), percolator, or paper filters. *(figure 6)*

CUTTING BOARDS Thin plastic cutting boards are great for chopping vegetables. They can be rolled up to pack neatly, and they can be trimmed to fit with other equipment. Consider keeping them in a separate stuff sack so they don't get sooty from the pots.

GRILLS AND FIREBOXES To cook over fire, you can either set up a basic grill or use a firebox. A basic grill rests on the rocks that you place in a ring around an open fire. You'll want to make sure that the grill is strong, stable and level so that you can confidently place large and possibly heavier pots on it over the fire. It's usually pretty easy to find a grill that you can bring on camping trips, but make sure it is built to handle heat.

Although you can cook over an open fire as just described, we recommend cooking over a firebox instead, for both environmental reasons and efficiency. The firebox is a relatively lightweight, folding metal box that contains your fire and has a sturdy grill on top. They come in various sizes, depending on how big a cooking area you want. The firebox also helps concentrate the heat from your fire, so it uses less wood and allows you to control the cooking temperature more accurately. Wearing a pair of leather work gloves, you can also pick it up while it's burning and move it to a new location if the wind shifts or rain starts. One of the biggest benefits of the firebox is that it doesn't leave a fire scar in sensitive environments or at campsites where there isn't a safe and established fire pit. In fact, many national parks require a firebox or 'fire pan' for any open fire. When it's time to break camp, you can use water to extinguish the ashes and to cool down the firebox before packing it away.

If space and weight isn't a concern you may even be able to bring a compact or collapsible hibachi and charcoal, or even a propane unit.

Tips!

The grill that comes with most fireboxes is prone to getting rusty and sooty so you may want to carry a different grill if you plan to barbeque.

LEFT A firebox doesn't leave a fire scar and lets you cook more efficiently by concentrating the heat of your fire.

STOVES Cook stoves work very well in all conditions. They can also help minimize your impact on high-traffic routes or ecologically sensitive areas because they leave no fire scar and they reduce or eliminate your use of firewood. Stoves are your only viable option in areas with insufficient wood. Even if you are predominantly using fire for cooking, carrying a lightweight compact stove (or several, depending on your group size) gives you a convenient backup and creates a safety buffer in case you find yourself in a situation where collecting wood and starting a fire is impractical. On a cold or wet day, having a stove along also makes it easy to quickly whip up a pot of soup, tea or hot chocolate at lunch time when you might not normally bother to build a fire. When the weather is chilly, warm fluids go a long way to keeping morale high.

There are many types of cook stoves available as single or double-burner units. The single units are very lightweight and compact. Double units, while bulkier, are typically less expensive than getting two single stoves. Some factors to consider when selecting a stove are things like maximum heat output, whether you can adjust the heat to allow simmering, weight, allowable type(s) of fuel, and your budget. Consult the manufacturer's specifications and talk to knowledgeable staff at specialty outdoor stores for technical information and to help you choose the right stove for your requirements.

Regardless of what stove you are using, you can always coax more heating power from your stove by sheltering it from wind. Optional windscreens are available for most stove models and worth bringing along.

If you're using stoves exclusively for a group of up to six people, plan to use a little less than a quart (about a liter) of fuel per day. Even with this guideline, it's a good idea to take an extra bottle, just in case. If you're using liquid fuel, bring a funnel to avoid spills when you refill the fuel bottles.

Tips!

Occasionally, stoves can require some field maintenance and there are specific repair kits for each brand of stove. Understanding how the stove works is the key to being able to fix or adjust them in the field, so take the time to read the user manual and test them before you're on a trip. When purchasing a stove, speak to a salesperson who can give you reliable, thorough advice.

LIQUID FUEL STOVES The more refined the fuel, the hotter and cleaner it will burn. Liquid fuel stoves that use naphtha (also known as white gas, Coleman fuel or shellite) are the hottest and most efficient stoves. Popular examples are the MSR WhisperLite and the Brunton Nova, although there are other comparable stoves offered by other manufacturers.

LEFT Cook stoves are compact and lightweight, which makes them the ideal solution when you need to travel light, are going to an ecologically sensitive area, or need backup for other trips.

All liquid fuel stoves work in basically the same way: the liquid fuel is pressurized with a pump and then forced out as a vapor through a small adjustable hole or jet. Once lit, adjusting the size of the jet increases or decreases the flame. On some stoves, after pressurizing the fuel with the pump, you may have to "prime" the stove by lighting a small amount of liquid fuel in the burner pan just below the jet. The heat from this small orange flame increases pressure in the brass fuel line and helps vaporize the fuel at the jet. Once lit, the heat from the stove will continue to pressurize and vaporize the fuel coming down the fuel line. Specific instructions for lighting and using a stove will vary depending on the type and model you choose, so read the manufacturer's documentation. If you have never used this type of stove before, practice lighting one outside a few times to get familiar with how it works before you take it on a trip.

In windy, cold or wet conditions, you can use a glob of starting paste (about the amount of toothpaste you use when brushing), which will burn for 20 seconds or so and help get things going.

There are usually specific fuel bottles that are designed to work with a particular stove. Because stoves depend on highly pressurized flammable materials, it is absolutely critical that all the pieces fit and work together perfectly. Always use the recommended fuel bottles.

MULTI-FUEL STOVES Multi-fuel stoves have an alternate fuel jet and will also burn less refined fuels such as kerosene or aviation gas. The ability to burn multiple types of gas is generally not required when camping in North America because white gas is usually not hard to find. However, if your camping and travel plans will bring you to areas where you are not sure of what types of fuels you will be able to purchase, you may wish to consider a multi-fuel stove.

LIQUEFIED PETROLEUM GAS STOVES Some stoves use Liquefied Petroleum Gas (LPG) in a canister that screws into the stove valve and lights easily. The canisters are not refillable but they can be recycled. They are lightweight and simple to use but bulkier than liquid fuel stoves and don't burn quite as hot.

METHYL ALCOHOL STOVES Another type of stove uses methyl alcohol as fuel. These stoves are simple to use, but do not produce as much heat and don't work as well in colder temperatures when alcohol does not vaporize effectively. These stoves are a reasonable backup but not recommended as your primary stove or cooking method. You are better off using a liquid fuel, multi-fuel or LPG stove.

BELOW Always test your stove before every trip.

LEFT The fuel canisters for an LPG stove are not refillable, and are bought separately from the stove unit.

THE DUTCH OVEN INNOVATION

Over the years, many guides and guests have traveled northern rivers as part of Black Feather trips. One of the most memorable, warm and hilarious of these was Fred Dawson from Orlando, Florida, who imparted to us a very important legacy. Before joining Black Feather as a client on ten or more northern trips over many summers, Fred had done a lot of canoe trips in the Quetico Park/Boundary Waters region, perfecting the art of Dutch oven cooking. When Fred first suggested that Black Feather adopt Dutch oven cooking, I was skeptical. It almost felt like he was suggesting we go back to the Dark Ages after years of innovation and fancy cooking gadgets, but he eventually wore me down and convinced me to bring three nesting Dutch ovens on our next Hood River trip. He had it all worked out. He had spent much of the winter sitting out in his garage in his upscale neighborhood in Florida, joking with curious neighbors, experimenting with recipes and determining the exact numbers of charcoal briquettes needed to obtain precisely 350°F for three stacked ovens. He did an impressive job and on the first night of the trip, on the shores of Contwoyto Lake, Fred served up a beautiful sirloin roast, a roasted vegetable medley, homemade rolls and a Sprite Cake for dessert. We were thoroughly impressed and ever since then, Dutch ovens have been a standard cooking tool on BF trips. (Fred's Dutch Oven Sprite Cake is one of the recipes included in this book.)

– Carolyn Pullen, Hood River 1994

BELOW The Dutch oven is our favorite way to bake.

OVENS Baking will vastly expand and improve the repertoire of meals you can create. All of these systems (and some better than others) can produce bread, cakes, casseroles and pies as perfectly as your oven at home. Each is simple to use and like the choice you'll have to make of whether to cook over stove or fire, each has its own advantages and idiosyncrasies.

DUTCH OVENS The Dutch oven is a fairly heavy cast aluminum or cast iron pot with a close-fitting lid. They stand on three legs that are about 2 inches (5 cm) high. The thick walls of the pot hold and evenly distribute heat. The heat source is charcoal or coals from the fire, and a reflective cover prevents the heat from escaping. They are too heavy and bulky for hiking but acceptable for canoeing and rafting trips, and you can also bring them sea kayaking if space and weight allows. Dutch ovens are our favorite outdoor ovens because they produce consistent results. We have provided detailed instructions for using them successfully in the next chapter, *Cooking Skills*.

OUTBACK OVENS This is a great lightweight system that bakes consistently well on a stove, but does not work very well over fire. It is light enough for hiking trips.

An Outback Oven consists of a Teflon-coated frying pan with a tight-fitting lid. Outback Ovens have a heat deflecting burner plate to prevent direct flame from burning the bottom of the food. A burn-resistant fabric hood goes over the pan like a tea cozy and distributes heat over the top of the pan. This hood can be used over other pots to heat water more quickly. A heat indicator on the lid helps to keep the heat consistent. It

RIGHT Mark Scriver slips the hood over the Outback Oven.

requires a stove with a separate fuel tank and burner because if the fuel tank is located under the hood, it could overheat. If the fuel tank overheats, it increases the pressure in the tank, which can result in an explosion, the tank bursting or an unpredictable flare-up. Don't let this happen.

Outback Ovens work best with a heat reflector that is the same diameter as the hood, so you may need to double up the regular MSR™ heat reflector. It will bake anything up to the depth of the pan (about 3.5 inches or 8 cm, not as deep as a Dutch oven or Coleman® Camp Oven). The more consistent the stove's heat output, the better. You may get some burning if your stove doesn't have a low enough or consistent heat adjustment.

CAMP OVENS

This folding box oven by Coleman® is designed to work on a two-burner stove but it also works well on an open fire. It is about 1 foot (30 cm) cubed, folds flat to about 2.5 inches (6 cm) thick, and comes with a rack that

LEFT Pizza coming out of the Camp Oven.

adjusts to three different levels. Although it has a temperature gauge that works well, if you use the Camp Oven over a fire, the gauge will become sooty and unreadable before long. Not to worry though, with a little experience you'll be able to guess at the temperature with reasonable accuracy. Camp Ovens will warp over time due to exposure to extreme heat, but they will keep on baking for years.

Camp Ovens are lighter than Dutch ovens, but require more attention and take up space over your fire or firebox. You can also use a Camp Oven over a stove, but it requires much more fuel than the Outback Oven.

REFLECTOR OVENS

Reflector ovens sit beside the fire to draw heat in at the bottom and out over the top of the pan. The oven folds flat and when assembled, it is about 1 foot by 1 foot by 1.5 feet (30 cm by 30 cm by 45 cm) with one shelf that can fit two pans side-by-side. You need a strong, consistent fire and it can be very challenging to keep the heat up if it is windy or cold. You also need to turn your pans periodically to get even heat. Many people swear by these but we find Dutch, Outback and Camp Ovens to be easier and more efficient.

POT OVENS AND DOUBLE BOILERS

For convenience, you can make your regular pots into pot ovens or double boilers. While pot ovens and double boilers work, it is often difficult to control the temperature and heat distribution and they produce inconsistent results. Again we recommend the use of Dutch, Outback, or Camp Ovens instead.

To make a pot oven, put three stones inside a big pot and place a smaller pot or pan (without a lid) on the stones. Put a lid on the big pot and put the whole thing over the fire. It works similarly to the Camp Oven in that heat from the fire should circulate around the big pot, so there is no need to put hot coals on top. However, it gets much less circulation than a Camp Oven does and gives uneven heat. If your pots are aluminum, you could even melt a hole in the pot.

For cakes or muffins that cook quickly or don't require as much heat, you can make your baking quite moist by using a double boiler. To make a double boiler, put water in the bottom of the big pot to prevent burning. Make sure the stones are big enough to keep the boiling water from splashing into the pan and that the water doesn't boil dry. The inside pan must be adequately smaller than the pot so that you can remove it at the end of the process.

OTHER EQUIPMENT There are a few more things you should bring along that will make your camp cooking run more smoothly.

GLOVES All-leather work gloves are an essential item for handling hot pots, moving the firebox, and packing up anything that is sooty.

FUEL BOTTLES A fuel bottle with a screw lid is significantly more secure than the containers that most fuel comes in, so it's a good idea to decant it into one of these better bottles.

LIGHTER AND MATCHES Lighters are essential items, so have a few extras in case some get lost, wet or run out of fuel. Matches, even waterproof ones, should be kept in a waterproof container. Do not rely on the "waterproofness" of waterproof matches.

SAWS A collapsible camp saw with a 12 to 15 inch (30 to 40 cm) blade is very useful for cutting firewood and for cutting poles to set up your tarp.

LEFT A folding saw is a handy piece of equipment around camp.

ABOVE Hand pumping water through a filter.

WATER TREATMENT Although the water in many of the lakes and rivers on which you'll find yourself camping is safe to drink untreated, you can never be certain that the water is free of viruses, pathogenic bacteria and protozoa that can cause significant digestive upset or illness. Even the most remote and clear streams can have them. Although some people will take the risk and drink untreated water on canoe trips, it's not a bad idea to treat all water before you drink it and there are several methods you can use.

BOILING Bringing water to a rolling boil is a great way to purify water because it reliably kills all viruses, pathogenic bacteria and protozoa. Just make sure the water comes to a full boil. The water you use in cooking doesn't need to be treated if it boils at some point during cooking.

FILTERS The most common and practical method of purifying water is by pumping water through a glass fiber or ceramic filter. This method usually eliminates most bad tastes. Depending on the model, you can expect to pump about a gallon (or liter) of water in 4 to 8 minutes. Glass fiber pumps are less expensive, but have a shorter lifespan (about 1,000 gallons). Ceramic filters will pump up to 2,500 gallons before the filter needs to be replaced. Some filters are designed to attach directly to water bottles and water bags, which makes filling these receptacles much easier.

To prolong the life of your filter and prevent bacteria from growing on it, always rinse your filter in chlorine-treated water after each trip and allow it to dry completely.

MIOX PURIFIER The Miox purifier combines non-iodized salt and a small amount of electricity from a battery to create an anti-oxidant that purifies water as effectively as chlorine. It is small, compact and self-sufficient.

CHLORINE Chlorine treatment, in tablet or liquid form, is a quick and easy way to treat drinking water for a group, and is available at any outdoor specialty store. The only downside is the distinctive chlorine taste that results.

Tips!

Staying hydrated is very important when you're exercising. To make your water extra tasty, add a fruity herbal teabag to the cold water in your water bottle in the morning. Remove it after five minutes and your water will have a subtle and refreshing berry or fruit flavor for the rest of the day. You can also add lemon or lime slices to your water; it tastes terrific and you get the added bonus of some vitamin C. Juice crystals are great at masking the taste of iodized water or other water treatment tablets but they are full of sugar and should be used in small quantities if possible. An option is to carry one bottle of juice and one of plain water so you can alternate throughout the day.

ABOVE While sea kayaks can carry a lot of weight, you'll often bring smaller, lighter equipment that fits more easily in the hatches.

EQUIPMENT CONSIDERATIONS FOR DIFFERENT TRIPS

The type of equipment you choose to bring will depend to some extent on the type of trip you are doing. We've outlined here what we consider the main factors that will affect how you pack, and what you bring on rafting, canoeing, kayaking and hiking trips.

RAFTING CONSIDERATIONS

In terms of equipment, rafting has the most flexibility because weight and space are not usually issues. In a raft, it might be possible to carry 20 lb propane tanks for stoves, folding tables and chairs, and coolers with ice to keep fresh or even frozen food for several days. You can plan a menu that uses a greater amount of fresh meats, dairy and produce if you have coolers that will keep it fresh. You can take heavier and bulkier items (as long as your trip doesn't involve much portaging) because the weight and storage capacity for a raft is far greater than for canoes and kayaks. Remember though, just because you *can* carry it, doesn't necessarily mean that you're better off having it. Having lots of carrying capacity reduces the need to pack efficiently, but your trip will probably run more smoothly if you're organized and your equipment list closely relates to what you need and will use.

CANOEING CONSIDERATIONS

Unless you're on a very long trip or in smaller canoes, you can take quite a bit of equipment and weight on a canoe trip, including some larger and more awkward items. Even on two and three week expeditions, you can take fresh vegetables and use heavier equipment such as a cooler, firebox, Dutch oven, and wannigan. (For more information about wannigans, see the section in Chapter 4 about *Equipment for Storing and Packing Food*.)

If your trip has a lot of portaging, you might lean towards lighter-weight and more compact equipment. Often when there are a lot of portages, it means you'll get to more remote and less populated areas, and many people consider it a badge of honor to get everything over portages in one trip. While it may be at the expense of more fresh food and more functional equipment (like a Dutch oven), you'll have to weigh the pleasures of being in the less-traveled places against the pleasures of taking those extra trips over the portage.

SEA KAYAKING CONSIDERATIONS

The carrying capacity of sea kayaks varies greatly depending on the type of boat. Tandem kayaks or 'expedition' model singles can carry as much or more per person than canoes, but the compartments are usually smaller so it can be difficult to carry large items. You will probably find yourself packing a lot of lightweight equipment more for its minimal volume and packing efficiency than the lightness it offers. Most sea kayak routes have little or no portaging so weight is not an issue. You will usually pack food in the front hatch compartment, which will be in contact with the water for most of the day, so fresh food will stay cool for longer.

HIKING CONSIDERATIONS

Hikers should be the most concerned with the weight and bulk of their food and equipment. On shorter trips, you might be tempted to take more than you need if there is leftover room in your pack. Just remember that your energy output and fatigue is directly proportional to the weight in your pack, so even on short trips it pays to carefully consider everything you take with you.

Mind you, it still can be nice to enjoy a few luxuries or equipment conveniences. Weight and gear trade-offs often boil down to a very personal and idiosyncratic science. One of our friends drilled holes in his toothbrush handle and would band saw off the margins of paperbacks to reduce weight, but still carried an espresso coffee maker.

COOKING SKILLS

CHAPTER 2

ABOVE On canoe trips, the bottom of an overturned canoe makes a great kitchen table.

Now that you've got all your outdoor cooking gear, it's time to learn how to set up a wilderness kitchen and use it.

CHOOSING A KITCHEN AREA Because it
naturally becomes a hub of social activity, many of your favorite camping memories will be from around the kitchen, so when you're choosing a campsite, give special consideration to the area where you'll be cooking. Try to satisfy as many aesthetic and functional factors as possible. These factors include: a good view, comfortable lounging, ease of setting up a tarp if the weather is inclement, proximity to a water source and proximity to the tent area.

Once you've staked out the kitchen area and erected a tarp (if necessary), you'll want to establish an area to set out and prepare the food. It is nice to have a raised work area or table where you can sit and keep the food and plates up off the ground. There are lightweight and collapsible tables available that are practical to carry if you're on a rafting trip. If you're on a beach, driftwood or beached logs will serve as tables and prevent sand from getting in the food and equipment. Large boulders or a rock shelf can also provide a comfortable work area, as well as shelter from winds. On canoe trips, you can use the bottom of an overturned canoe. By propping the upside-down canoe up with spare food barrels, rocks or logs, or by digging the ends down into a gravel or sand bar, you can quickly transform it into a spacious table.

However you choose to set up your kitchen area, do your best to keep it as clean as possible. Not only is a clean kitchen more hygienic, but it will go a long way towards keeping unwanted, four-legged visitors away.

CHOOSING A HEAT SOURCE–FIRE OR STOVE

When you become familiar with using a wood fire or one of several types of stoves, you'll be able to keep the heat consistent and predictable, and turn out culinary masterpieces as easily as you would in a kitchen at home. The type of cooking method you use will be determined by your method of travel, where you are traveling, as well as your personal preference for fires or stoves.

COOKING WITH FIRE

Fires have a great aesthetic appeal and are hard to beat for sheer heat output. As long as you have a good supply of firewood, you can take as long as you want to cook and enjoy the comfort of the fire late into the night. However, it can be both impractical and environmentally unsound to collect firewood where trees are scarce and in heavily traveled areas. In some areas there may be temporary or permanent restrictions on fires or collecting firewood. In wet conditions, starting and maintaining an efficient fire can be challenging, but we'll give you some helpful suggestions for that.

For many people, a campfire is an essential part of the camping experience. It raises morale in nasty weather, provides warmth on a cold day, dries clothes and offers hours of entertainment for those who like to poke and prod as well as those who prefer to simply gaze at the fire's ever-changing tapestry of light. There's something very comforting about the warmth you feel while tending the fire and preparing your meal, the pleasant smells of burning wood and cooking food, and the occasional sting of smoke in your eyes.

SETTING UP AN OPEN FIRE

If you're cooking over an open fire and using an established fire pit, make sure that there isn't any chance of the fire reaching a root or even the active layer of soil. (The active layer of soil is where all the bacteria live that keep soil healthy and cause organic matter to biodegrade). If you have to build a fire pit, try to build it on rock or sand, which will be the safest and also cause the least environmental damage. You can use rocks around the fire to shelter it from the wind, concentrate the heat, keep flames and sparks from spreading, and to support a grill about 7 to 9 inches (15 to 20 centimeters) above the ground.

SETTING UP A FIREBOX

If you are cooking using a firebox, similar concerns need to be addressed as for an open fire.

RIGHT If you're setting up an open fire, it is safest and has the least impact on the environment if you build the fire pit on rock or sand.

If there is an existing fire pit, modify the rocks to form a U-shape that the firebox will fit inside. While you are at this task, make sure that you clean up any bits of foil or garbage that may have been caught between the stones. Make sure that the open end of the firebox corresponds with the open end of the U. If there is not an existing fire pit, you can choose the site best suited to the task. Ideally you can find a rock, sand, dirt or gravel base to prevent heat from damaging any vegetation. If this is not possible, choose an area with minimal vegetation. Make sure that you check for overhead branches. You will also want to place your firebox in an area that allows for good traffic flow in and around the cooking area.

SELECTING FIREWOOD

Whether you'll be cooking over an open fire or using a more environmental firebox, before starting a fire you'll need to gather some firewood... and a good fire needs good wood. Cooking over a fire with poor quality or insufficient wood can be slow and frustrating. Taking the time to gather good quality wood can be therapeutic and lead you on interesting adventures. At well-used campsites, it may be better to paddle to another shore to gather wood. On some northern trips, where wood is more sparse, we gather bits as we see it from about lunchtime onward. By the time we stop to camp, each canoe looks like a floating beaver lodge.

The biggest mistake is using wood that isn't dry enough. For environmental and practical reasons, never cut any live trees. Dead and fallen branches, driftwood or entire dead saplings are fair game. If you brought a collapsible saw, you can collect and use wood more efficiently. Avoid cutting dead lower branches from trees close to the campsite or from anywhere that will have a visual impact. The best indication of suitable dryness is that the bark has fallen off. Wood found on the ground and that has lost its bark will dry quickly, even after a rainstorm, and it is also less likely to have rot. The heat for cooking will be easier to control if you use wood no thicker than about 3 inches (6 cm) in diameter.

STARTING A FIRE

Starting a fire is a quintessential outdoor skill. It can teach you about science, patience and life itself. (If you doubt this, read *To Build a Fire* by Jack London).

Remove the grill from the firebox or fire pit, and start with toothpick-sized dry twigs in a bundle the size of your wrist. Get it as compact as possible. You can use paper or birch bark (only from deadfall) to help start the fire or simply hold a lighter or match to the bundle of small twigs. They will catch fire quickly but the bundle needs to produce enough heat to ignite larger sticks. Gradually add larger and larger pieces of wood until the firebox is full or the fire pit has enough wood

LEFT The best place to set up a firebox is on a flat rock or sand.

to get a manageable blaze going. At first you'll need to shelter your fire from the wind but once it's established, let some breeze in to give the fire more oxygen.

Once the fire is started, heap on lots of wood and put as many pots of water as you need or can fit. Hot water can be used to make warm drinks, soup or to rehydrate dehydrated meals, and any water left over can be poured into drinking bottles when it has cooled.

Tips!

If you are having trouble starting the twigs, you can use a small tea light candle, fire paste or wax fire starter cubes which can provide enough heat to dry and ignite damp tinder or twigs. Thin strips of birch bark catch easily and do provide some heat if you separate the layers of bark and add it to the twig bundle. Only use birch bark that you find lying on the ground; never peel it off the tree.

WET WEATHER If you're stuck with rain-soaked wood, use a knife to remove the damp outer wood and then shave off thin strips of dry wood to start the fire. In wet weather, take extra care to collect good quality wood even if it is wet. Wood that is a bit "punky" or rotten soaks up rainwater and will be a detriment to your fire. Once the fire is going, have a few sticks drying on top of the grill to add later.

REALLY WET WEATHER If you are having trouble starting a fire, you might use one of the following techniques. One option is to use some of your stove fuel. It's yet another reason to carry a stove as backup even if you're planning on using fire for most of the cooking. The other option is to use commercially available fire paste or fire sticks. You can even carry a small "tea light" candle, which can provide enough flame and heat to allow damp tinder to get started. Even if you are using fuel or other fire starters to help start the fire, you need to build your fire carefully in order to get the wood burning efficiently and safely. Start in the same way as described above, with a bundle of small sticks. Pile on some bigger sticks. If you are using a bit of stove fuel, pour on a few splashes. You should need less than a half a cup. If you need more than that, you might as well just use the stove. Make sure that you're getting some fuel on all the wood including the smallest twigs. Be sure to close the fuel bottle and move it well away from the fire. White gas is highly flammable so use caution when lighting it. You can light a piece of birch bark or paper and toss it into the twigs and wood that you have prepared. The vapors and flames rise fast, so you're safest keeping low and to the side of the fire. The idea is that the heat from the burning fuel will dry the wood and ignite the small twigs. Never add fuel to a fire that has already been lit. Even if the fire appears to be out, the smallest ember can cause an explosion or potentially ignite the fuel before it leaves your hand.

CONTROLLING THE HEAT It is easiest to control the heat of a fire if you have a good bed of coals. Then when you add wood, it will catch quickly and raise the heat. If you have too much heat, you can remove a couple of sticks or rearrange

LEFT The best wood to use for cooking is dry, no thicker than 3 inches (6 cm) in diameter, found on the ground, and has lost its bark.

and slightly scatter the coals. With good wood and a bit of experience, you can control the heat of a fire as well as you can with any conventional stove or oven. In the evening or when breaking camp, let the fire burn down so that you don't have to put out a lot of half-burned wood.

TINFOIL COOKING With some tinfoil and a fire of hot coals, you can bake fish, potatoes and other vegetables. Put a bit of oil on the tinfoil so the food won't stick. Potatoes and yams can be washed and wrapped in a single layer of foil and placed directly in the coals. Turn them frequently to avoid burning and cook for 45 minutes. They will cook more evenly if you put them on the grill of a firebox. Squash is prepared the same way after the seeds have been removed. Vegetables such as potatoes, carrots and onions can also be sliced and wrapped in two layers of foil with seasonings and butter or oil to make them cook faster. Carefully seal all the edges and try not to perforate the foil to make sure that the moisture stays in and steams the food. Fish is delicious steamed and baked the same way. Sprinkle the gutted cavity with spices, lemon and onions and wrap the fish in two layers of tinfoil. Thirty minutes or so will cook a 2-3 lb (1 kg) fish over a medium fire. The juices steam the fish and the skin peels away with the tinfoil.

BARBEQUE Barbequing is great way to cook food in the outdoors because it's healthy and tastes great. Fireboxes are ideal for barbequing but you can also do it over a grill on an open fire. Build up a good supply of coals using hardwood if possible, because their coals will last longer. Metal or wooden skewers will keep vegetables or small pieces of meat organized on the grill and prevent them from falling through.

RIGHT Skewers of fresh-caught fish are grilled up for dinner.

You can barbeque vegetables, fish, meat and even corn on the cob (just leave the husks on). Because it is hard to cook other things on the fire when you're grilling food, it's good to have a stove along so that you can make other dishes like rice.

DEEP FRYING On a day hike from the Mountain River, our group somehow got talking about onion rings and French fries. I forget what we had planned for supper, but we ended up giving into the craving and making an entire meal of onion rings and fries, as well as veggies in tempura batter on crackers with cream cheese. On another trip with that same group, we made poutine, the French-Canadian classic made by melting cheese and pouring gravy on fries.

A wok or small pot is great for deep frying. For the best results, use oils like peanut oil, corn oil or safflower oil that will heat to the required temperature of around 365°F without smoking and breaking down.

You will have good success deep frying potatoes, yams, garlic and onions. Fish or hard cheese can be coated with seasoned flour or cornmeal and deep fried. With a thin tempura batter, you could try deep frying mushrooms, onions, fish, sushi rolls and egg rolls. Remove any excess moisture on vegetables before frying.

Exercise caution around the hot oil, which can catch fire or burn you if it splatters. Use lots of oil so that whatever you cook can float freely in the oil, and cook in small batches to keep the temperature constant. Always heat the oil before adding the food. If the oil is below the ideal temperature, the food will absorb too much oil and become soggy rather than crispy. It's also a good idea to put pieces of roughly the same size in each batch so that they take about the same amount of time to cook.

Although not necessary, it is recommended that you place fried food on paper or paper towel as it comes out of the pot to soak up excess oil. When you're finished cooking, the oil can be cooled, strained and reused.

COOKING WITH STOVES Cooking with stoves in the outdoors can be more complicated than turning a dial on your range at home, but as you get more familiar with them, you can cook with the same finesse on a camp stove that you would at home. The most common types of stoves are described in the section about *Equipment*. This section will describe how to use them.

Although it almost goes without saying, for the sake of safety and efficiency, make sure you know how to operate and even perform basic maintenance on your stove before leaving for your trip. This may come as a surprise to some, but the owner's manual is made for this purpose. While stove malfunction is not very common, consider packing a photocopy of the guide in a waterproof bag in case you need to do any troubleshooting in the field.

Heat from the stove is more concentrated than heat from a fire. To avoid burning food, you should stir liquids more often than you would for a fire. You can also use a heat diffuser such as the one that comes with the Outback Oven. You can improve the efficiency of a stove by using a non-flammable pot cover that keeps the lid and upper pot from losing heat especially in cold or windy weather.

Some stoves lack a reliable control of the heat output and do not simmer well. If you are using stoves exclusively you may want at least one of your stoves to have this ability, especially for cooking sauces or baking.

SETTING UP A STOVE There are several criteria for a perfect stove location. The stove should have a stable base so that it won't tip over easily. If your stove has a separate burner plate, don't put it on something that will burn, melt or be damaged by the heat. For example, even if it doesn't burn surrounding plants and moss, heat from the stove may rob these living things of vital moisture, so keep the stove away from vegetation. It's also important to set up the stove where it will be sheltered, but not so much that the tank will be heated by the stove burner or where there is inadequate ventilation. From a safety perspective, it also shouldn't be in a confined area in case of flare-ups. A flat rock, out of the way of pedestrian traffic, is usually perfect.

Safety Tips!

Stoves produce carbon monoxide and should be used only in well-ventilated areas. Never operate a stove in your tent or a closed vestibule.

COOKING WITH ALCOHOL STOVES This is a simple technology. An open container of alcohol vaporizes and if you light the surface, it will provide a moderate heat. If you shelter and focus the heat, you will be able to boil water. This is a good supplemental heat source but difficult to use as a main cooking source.

COOKING WITH LIQUEFIED PETROLEUM GAS STOVES Liquefied Petroleum Gas (LPG) stoves use a pressurized canister of butane or propane. Simply connect the canister to the stove burner, turn on the flow of gas and ignite. They are simple and usually dependable but the canisters are bulky. These stoves don't match the heat output of the liquid fuel stoves.

COOKING WITH LIQUID FUEL STOVES These stoves are the most practical for most outdoor trips. There are more parts to this stove, some of which require maintenance

and occasional repair or replacement. The liquid fuel is pressurized with a pump. Thirty or forty pumps will usually provide adequate pressure. Make sure there is enough air in the tank to be pressurized. Most stoves have a maximum fill line leaving an inch or so of air in the tank. Occasionally the plastic parts on some of these pumps break or the gasket needs to be replaced so carrying a complete replacement pump is a good idea on long trips.

The pressurized vapor in the tank is released through a small adjustable hole or jet. Sometimes dirt or soot can clog this small opening. You can clean this when the stove is off by shaking it upside down or pushing a tiny wire through the small opening.

On some stoves, after pressurizing the fuel with the pump, you may have to "prime" the stove by lighting a small amount of liquid fuel in the burner pan just below the jet. The heat from this small orange flame increases pressure in the brass fuel line and helps vaporize the fuel at the jet. When there is adequate pressure and the stove is operating efficiently, it will burn with a blue flame. Specific instructions for lighting and using a stove will vary depending on the type and model you choose, so read the manufacturer's documentation.

In windy, cold or wet conditions, you can use a glob of starting paste (about the amount of toothpaste you use when brushing), which will burn for 20 seconds or so and help get things going.

Once lit, the heat from the stove will continue to pressurize the tank and vaporize the fuel coming down the fuel line. You

LEFT Cooking with an Outback Oven.

ABOVE Lighting a liquid fuel stove.

may coax a bit more output by pumping the tank just after the stove is lit (especially if it is full) or when the tank is almost empty. You may also lose pressure in very cold temperatures so keep the tank off snow or very cold ground. While low pressure in the tank can affect the efficiency too much pressure is a danger.

Safety Tips!

Do not allow heat from the stove to come in contact with the fuel tank. The result is increased pressure in the tank which can burst the tank and cause an explosion or unpredictable flare-up. If you're using a large pot or griddle or if you're using a windscreen or heat reflector, make sure the fuel tank is not being heated. Windscreens and heat reflectors are used to focus the stove output on the pots and isolate the heat from the fuel tank.

USING FUEL TANKS For stoves that do not have an integral fuel tank, always use the fuel bottles that are designed to be used with that stove. Because stoves depend on highly pressurized flammable materials, it is absolutely critical that all the pieces fit and work together perfectly. If a fuel bottle gets dented, it may weaken the wall so do not use it as a fuel tank for the stove.

When refueling the tank, the stove should be off and away from other open flames. Be sure to close the extra fuel bottles before relighting the stove. Use a funnel to avoid spillage.

If you're using stoves exclusively for a group of up to six people, plan to use a little less than a quart (about a liter) of fuel per day, plus a little extra, just in case. Since you'll have a limited amount of fuel, you will want to plan your menu and the cooking order to use the fuel and cooking time wisely.

COOKING WITH OVENS In this section we'll describe how to get the most out of the type of oven that you've brought along.

COOKING WITH DUTCH OVENS For the best results with a Dutch oven, you'll need a thick pair of all-leather work gloves, a pair of tongs, some charcoal briquettes and some tinfoil. We recommend heavy-duty foil because if you treat it well, you can reuse it more times than regular foil and reduce waste. Remember to recycle the foil when you get back.

As you're preparing your dish in a separate pan, put the briquettes on the grill of a firebox for about 4 minutes to get them burning. You'll need about 20 briquettes for the average large oven. Lay a piece of tinfoil on a bare flat rock or sand. While the briquettes are starting to burn, heat the Dutch oven slightly, oil the inside, add your batter, dough, or main course ingredients, and put the lid on. When the briquettes are glowing on one side, put on your leather gloves, use the tongs to place ten briquettes on the foil, and then set the oven on top of the briquettes. The oven legs keep the oven from touching the briquettes and will allow the heat to distribute evenly. Put ten briquettes on top of the oven. Wrap tinfoil around the oven and close it up to keep the heat in. If you don't crush the tinfoil up too much, you should be able to reuse it several times. When you think the dish is ready, unwrap the foil and take the lid off carefully to avoid getting ashes in the food.

If you're running low on briquettes, you can use coals from the fire but they don't put out heat as consistently or for as long. While it is possible to cook with a Dutch oven over a slow fire, and put coals or burning sticks on top, this method is less reliable, requires constant attention and takes up a cooking spot over your fire. The briquette/tinfoil method is our preferred method of baking. Dutch ovens with charcoal briquettes may be the bulkiest, but it is also the one of the most consistent methods we know of.

COOKING WITH TWO DUTCH OVENS It is most efficient to bake with two Dutch ovens at the same time. You can get Dutch ovens in different sizes so that one nests inside the other for packing. With large groups you may need to use both for the same dish, but with groups as large as eight, you can use one oven to bake a main course lasagna and the other for a dessert, or one for a dessert and the other to make some kind of bread for the next day's lunch.

You'll need about 26 briquettes for two ovens, compared to 20 for a single large one, which is why baking two dishes at once is more efficient. Set up the large Dutch oven exactly as you would if it were the only one, but before you wrap it in

RIGHT Double Dutch.

ABOVE SEQUENCE Dutch ovens produce the most consistent results for baking in a camp kitchen. They are terrific for making breads and cakes.

tinfoil, put the second oven on top of it. The final six briquettes go on top of the second oven. Wrap tinfoil around both ovens, put another piece on top, and close it up to keep the heat in.

COOKING WITH OUTBACK OVENS

Outback Ovens allow you to make great baked goods provided you are cooking over a backpacking stove. They do not work with a two-burner stove. Your best bet is a single-burner stove that allows a simmer mode. Simply mix up your raw ingredients and put them into the pan of the Outback Oven. Light your stove, then put the heat baffle over the flame, which disperses the heat. Then put your pan on the heat baffle, put the lid on the pan and cover the pan and baffle with the insulating and reflective cover. Keep the stove on low and cook according to directions. Most items are done in about 20 minutes. You can cook main courses, such as quiche, pizza, calzone and chicken pot pie. The Outback Oven shines with goodies such as quick breads, muffins, cakes, brownies and cinnamon buns.

Tips!

Do not fill the Outback Oven too full with your baking – it's better to make two batches than to have your baking overflow as it cooks.

COOKING WITH CAMP OVEN

Coleman® Camp Ovens usually come with one rack that is adjustable to three different heights. If you want to bake two pans at once, you can use something like a piece of fencing wire or even a modified wire coat hanger as a bottom rack, which will pull the sides in and help to keep the rack in place. If you're careful with the heat you can bake a third pan on the very bottom of the oven.

While you can use a stove with a Camp Oven, it takes quite a bit of fuel and it's usually easier over a fire, especially using a firebox. To get a consistent heat source from fire under the oven, set up a good bed of coals at one end of the firebox with only a few sticks producing low flames. Have a well-stoked fire at the other end of the firebox so that you can add coals from it to the bed of coals under the oven as you cook. If you add fresh sticks directly under the Camp Oven, they will usually flame up and burn the bottom of the baking pans. If you are afraid the fire will still be too hot, you can place a pan of sand or water in the bottom of the oven to help diffuse the heat from the fire.

LEFT Potatoes being baked in the Camp Oven.

ABOVE Fresh-caught fish from the Pacific Ocean on a sea kayaking trip.

PREPARING FRESH FISH
Whether fishing is the main purpose of your trip or a last-minute thought, wilderness tripping usually offers great fishing opportunities in rarely fished waters. Some people prefer to catch and release, but fresh fish is an excellent supplement to your menu. Make sure you carry appropriate fishing licenses and check for local information about locations, species, lures and flies.

If there are bears in your area, remember that they like fish too! With a few simple precautions you can avoid inadvertently inviting them to dinner. Always clean your hands after handling fish, and be careful about where you clean fish. It's best to clean and gut or fillet fish far away from your campsite. You can also do it on a rock or piece of wood at the shoreline, then throw the rock into the water or burn the wood afterwards, and dump the entrails and head in the water, deep enough that other campers won't see the remains.

Fish seem to taste best when they go from the water to the pan... or even directly to your plate in the form of sushi or sashimi. If you need to save a fish for later, gut or fillet it and put it in a plastic bag so that it's ready for the next meal. Gutting a fish takes less time to do but the fish will typically take longer to cook than a fish that has been filleted. Your choice will depend on your time constraints, your preferences, and the recipe you've chosen.

Dorsal

Dorsal Fin

Caudal Fin

Pectoral Fin

Anterior

Posterior

Mouth

Gill Flap

Anal Fin

Pelvic Fin

Ventral

Fish Parts

Tips!

Fish tastes better if you cut the gills and bleed the fish almost immediately after you catch and kill it. You can usually do this right from your boat if you happen to be in one. Let the blood drip into the water so that it won't attract animals.

FISH PARTS If you know the parts of a fish, it will be easier to follow the instructions below for gutting, cleaning and filleting.

GUTTING AND CLEANING METHOD The simplest way to prepare a fish for frying or baking is to gut it and remove the gills, and then, if you wish, remove the head. It's a good idea to remove the scales when you're cleaning a fish, even if you're not going to eat the skin.

Step 1: Scaling Hold the tail of the fish and with the angle of your knife blade perpendicular to the fish's skin, scrape from the tail toward the head with light pressure. The clear scales you remove from the side of the fish will usually be less than half an inch (12 mm) in diameter, depending on the type of fish. Scrape the entire skin including the belly where the scales are smaller, then rinse the fish to wash the scales off. Scales can be really hard to see, so rinse the fish well.

Step 2: Gutting Make an incision along the belly of the fish from the bone behind the gills and pectoral fins to and around the "vent" by the anal fin. If you want to remove the head, slice behind the gill covers and the pectoral fins and right through the backbone. (You can also leave the head on for aesthetic reasons or to cook the delicious cheek flesh found just behind the eye.) Next, remove the gills, gill covers and pectoral fins. Remove all the entrails inside the ribcage. Slice through and remove the blood vessels near the spine and with your knife perpendicular, scrape the membranes inside the ribcage. Follow this up with a good rinse, and your fish is ready to cook.

Step 3: Cooking You can bake or steam your fish wrapped in tinfoil, barbeque it on the grill, or fry it in a pan or griddle. If you are frying bigger fish, cook it more slowly and cover with a lid or tinfoil so the thick middle section has a chance to cook. It's always an option to stuff the fish with something tasty before wrapping it in foil, like onions and butter.

When the fish is cooked through, the flesh should separate easily from the backbone and rib cage. Grasp the backbone near the head in one hand and the tail in the other, then lift the backbone gently. A third hand with a fork can help to separate the flesh from the backbone and skeleton on one side. Flip the fish over and lift the intact backbone again and remove the flesh from the ribcage on the other side of the fish. Some fish have another row of bones but this method will remove most of the bones for most fish.

ABOVE Cleaning and filleting the fish on the water is the surest way to keep the smell of fish out of your campsite.

FILLETING METHOD Filleting removes the meat from the backbone on each side of the fish. It requires a knife with a sharp, long and flexible blade (as well as a bit of patience) but you end up with a thin piece of meat with few bones that is faster to cook than a gutted fish. You can easily remove the skin with this method so there is no need to remove the scales first unless you prefer to leave the skin on. (If you want to leave the skin on, scale it first as described above under *Gutting and Cleaning*.) It isn't really worth filleting small fish because the meat along the ribcage will be so thin. Techniques vary, but this is one that we know and use:

Step 1: Filleting the Top of the First Side

With a sharp knife (and sharp is key) make an incision along the back of the fish on one side of the dorsal fin. Your objective is to make the incision so that your knife can run along the dorsal bones from the head toward the tail of the fish.

To separate the flesh from the dorsal bones, slice a little bit at a time with your blade angled toward the dorsal bones so you can feel them with the blade, and guide the knife edge along the top of them from head to tail. Keep slicing the blade from head to tail and gradually separate the flesh from the bones until all the flesh between the top of the fish and the backbone has been removed from the dorsal bones.

RIGHT A filleting competition.

Step 2: Filleting the Tail and Backbone

Because the ribcage ends behind the anal fins, there are no bones between the anal fins and the tail, so you can slice right through the fish from the top to the bottom. With your blade angled toward the backbone, and holding the head, continue with a sawing motion to the tail.

Now cut toward the backbone from the tail to just behind the gills and pectoral fin.

Step 3: Filleting the Top of the Second Side

With the fillet detached except for the ribcage, repeat Step 1 and Step 2 for the other side.

Step 4: Filleting the Ribcage

Slice a little bit at a time with the blade angled toward the ribs, which will leave the bones intact. The trick is to remove the flesh while leaving the bones from the ribcage behind. Repeat this on the other side and you'll end up with two fillets with the skin attached.

Step 5: Removing the Skin

To remove the skin, put the fillet skin-down on a cutting board. Hold the skin near the tail tightly, and slice between the skin and the flesh at the tail end of the fillet, working toward the head. Work the knife back and forth with the blade on a slight angle toward the skin and putting pressure toward the cutting board. Here is where a long flexible blade is essential. The skin will neatly part from the flesh leaving you with very few bones. On some fish, like pike, there is another row of bones running from the backbone into the flesh but filleting still makes the fish easier to cook and serve.

LEFT Cutting from the tail to just behind the gills and pectoral fin.

FOOD HANDLING AND SANITATION

If you follow a couple of easy routines and principles, it is easy to maintain a clean and sanitary kitchen area. Everyone has different standards of hygiene at home so it's a great idea to meet and discuss procedures for food handling, hygiene and managing waste both food and human at the beginning of the trip. It's even better if the group has already touched on these fundamental issues during a trip planning meeting so that everyone starts out the trip with the same expectations and is able to come prepared.

Most wilderness environments have fewer germs than our homes (other than animal feces and garbage left by inconsiderate campers) so by managing our food and waste properly, it is easy to stay healthy.

HAND WASHING Washing hands is the easiest way to control the spread of germs. If everyone washes their hands before eating or handling food and after going to the bathroom, everyone will stay healthy. If it is convenient to wash hands, most people will; if it's a hassle, many people will forget.

A very simple system is to fill a "dromedary" water bag with water and have a bar of soap or squeeze bottle with hand soap and a hand towel. Hang it near the kitchen so it is easy to wash hands before eating or helping with food preparation. This system is preferable to a wash basin, because dirty water left in the basin can possibly spread germs to others who wash in the same water. When you pack up your gear for the day, keep the hand-washing bag with the lunch so you can fill it before any of the lunch preparations begin. At a campsite, leave the toilet paper and trowel kit near the hand-washing station to remind people to wash up after using the bathroom kit. (There's more information about the bathroom kit in the section about *Managing Waste*.)

Tips!

You can achieve superhero status on cold mornings by filling the hand-washing water bag with heated water.

Antibacterial soap has become very popular in recent years, but many people don't realize that it is not really necessary to get clean, unless you are scrubbing up to perform surgery. The major disadvantage of antibacterial soap is that it is not good for the environment, introducing chemicals that can upset fragile ecosystems. You will kill all the bacteria on your hands with normal soap and a reasonable amount of rubbing. If you feel the need to sterilize your hands, use alcohol-based antibacterial hand sanitizer that works by just rubbing it into your hands until it is dry. These sanitizers can be very convenient on camping trips and will satisfy the hygiene requirements of the most fastidious in your group. It's a great idea to keep waterless hand sanitizer or disposable wipes with the toilet kit for use after bathroom breaks during the day or before snacks.

RIGHT A water bag that pours a small stream of fresh water is better than a basin where dirty water is reused and germs can spread.

FOOD WASHING AND HANDLING Rinse and dry any produce at home before packing it so that you don't have to wash it on your trip. If food must be rinsed at a campsite for any reason, you can use clean untreated water if the food is going to be boiled, but if it is going to be eaten raw, wash it in filtered or treated water.

Use clean utensils, plates and cutting boards when preparing food for cooking. You don't have to wash them in between cutting produce or cheese but anything that has touched uncooked meat shouldn't touch other food without being washed first.

SPILLS AND LEFTOVERS Clean up any spilled food so it doesn't make a sticky mess, spread germs or attract animals. Leftovers can be saved in a plastic bag for another meal or sealed in a plastic bag and put in the garbage. Reuse plastic bags from the packed food and bring along a few spare and sturdy bags in case you run out. Keep the leftover food and garbage separated from the food to prevent spoilage. For more information about garbage, refer to the section about *Managing Waste*.

WASHING DISHES
The best way to wash dishes in camp is just like you would at home, in hot soapy water, and then rinse them separately in hot water. If you put a big pot of water on to heat up as soon as the meal comes off the fire or stove, you'll have dishwater ready when everyone is finished eating. You'll need something for scrubbing, a biodegradable soap, a flat surface (like the bottom of the canoe,) as well as two, big, clean pots. Although any pots will do, there are collapsible camp sinks made of coated material that work really well for the job.

Before dropping your dishes into the wash pot, scrape off all the scrap food on to a hot fire or into the garbage. This step will help your wash water go a lot further. When you're finished with the dishwater, pour it in a "gray water" hole. A gray water hole is a small hole dug into the active layer of soil, at least 50 feet (about 20 meters) from shore and at least as far from camp. Because it is dug into the active layer of soil, the tiny food particles and soap you deposit there will biodegrade more easily. If there are pieces of food debris in the water, pour it through a strainer and then throw the contents of the strainer into the fire or garbage.

Let the dishes air dry on the hull of an overturned canoe (if you have one along) or on a flat rock before packing them away. Air drying is the most hygienic and happily requires the least work.

On longer trips, it's a good idea to wash out the cutlery apron, the wannigan or any of the barrels that get dirty.

LEFT With two collapsible sinks, you can have a wash station and a rinse station.

It is important to understand that even biodegradable soap or food bits will have an effect on a sensitive aquatic ecosystem, not to mention detract from the next camper's experience, so never wash your dishes in the lake or river. "Biodegradable soap" means it biodegrades in soil where the bacteria and enzymes exist to break it down, not in water. If you just have a few non-greasy dishes, you can wash them in a pot of cold water and then dump the water in a hole in the active layer of soil.

Tips!

For larger groups, or if you are leading a commercial trip as a guide, a three-stage wash is recommended. The first pot is with hot, soapy water, the second is with hot water with a few drops of bleach added for sterilization, and the third is a warm or cold water rinse.

MANAGING WASTE

When camping, there is nothing more distasteful than encountering the waste of past campers. If you're going to camp, you need to manage your waste properly. There are three types of waste you'll be responsible for: garbage, food waste, and human waste.

GARBAGE AND FOOD WASTE

There are two options for dealing with garbage and food waste, which will include both the garbage that you generate and the garbage that you will unfortunately find along your travels. (If others before you were careless, you can at least feel good about being part of the solution and not the problem.) The two options are to burn it or to pack it out. If you've packed well for your trip, you really should have very little garbage and food waste to burn or pack out. You can minimize your food waste by being fairly accurate about quantities when planning your menu, but you'll still have compost from fresh vegetables and leftovers.

Note: Although burying your food waste will often seem like the most convenient thing to do, we *strongly* discourage you from doing it. Animals of all kinds will smell the buried garbage and dig it up. Animals that get used to scavenging human food usually become "problem animals" that hang around campsites and gradually lose their fear of humans. Bears in particular (although they naturally avoid humans) can become a serious nuisance or a danger if they become accustomed to human food, and under these circumstances have to be destroyed by wildlife officials.

PACKING IT OUT If you're not using fires on your trip, or you don't want to burn your garbage, use the plastic bags that you've saved from your food to pack out the garbage. Use firm knots and double-bag anything moist that might leak. You might bring along a few spare bags of various sizes for garbage but usually you'll have extra bags available after the first meal.

There are several disadvantages to using a single large garbage bag: it means more weight and combined moisture, it is more likely to tear and leak, and it won't fit in as many places, especially on sea kayaking and hiking trips. For these reasons we recommend using several smaller bags.

For garbage that will be packed out, we use a three-bag system: one for "real" garbage which cannot be recycled (which includes food waste that we might not burn), one for clean and crushed cans and clean bottles, and one for clean plastics. The contents of the last two bags can be recycled at the end of the trip. Keep these bags well separated from the food so the garbage won't spread bacteria.

The best way to deal with empty cans and their sharp lids is to wash them out or burn them to eliminate any smells, drop the lids into the bottom of the cans, and then crush the cans so they take up less space in the recycling bag, and the lids can't slip out and slice anything. Be careful of sharp edges when you wash the cans. If there are any sharp bits sticking out, or lids that did not get crushed in the bottom of cans, be aware that these can tear the bag they're in as well as the other garbage bags, so pack the cans separately or in a protected place.

Plastic garbage materials that cannot be cleaned and eventually recycled should be packed out and put in land fill sites rather than burned where toxic gases are released into the environment. However, if you have plastics that would be particularly

ABOVE With a few precautions you can prevent unwanted visitors from helping themselves to your food.

attractive to wild animals, such as greasy bacon wrappings, you might consider burning these few things over a very hot fire.

Moist garbage such as pasta, oatmeal or stews goes in the bag for "real garbage"; just make sure the bags are sturdy, and well-sealed. For very wet garbage like leftover soup, dilute it, pour it through a strainer to catch the big chunks and then pour the waste water into the "gray water" hole (discussed above in the section on *Washing Dishes*). Another solution for really wet garbage is to add a powdered product that gels the liquid waste, encapsulates the solid waste, removes odors and begins the decay process. As a guideline, about a half cup of this stuff will neutralize five cups of cream of mushroom soup. It is not necessary for all of the wet garbage you are packing out, but nice to have for the particularly messy leftovers.

BURNING FOOD WASTE AND GARBAGE The evening is the best time to burn your food waste, when you can do it on a hot fire and let the material burn completely. At breakfast and lunch, bag the burnable garbage (like vegetable waste) for the evening fire or simply pack it out. It is easier to burn garbage on a firebox than on an open fire because you can put it on the grill where it will dry out and burn rather than smother the fire. It will save burning time and wood if you chop up the compost into smaller pieces.

BELOW Burning food waste at the end of a meal.

HUMAN WASTE There is nothing that will detract from your wilderness experience more than seeing used toilet paper. Human waste rules will vary depending on where you are visiting, and these rules will usually take into account the type of ecosystem and the kind of traffic the area sees. Find out what they are by contacting park or natural resource officials so that you can manage human waste in an environmentally responsible way.

In some parks and in well-traveled areas, outdoor pit toilets are provided. If they are available, be sure to use them. In some very high traffic areas that are ecologically sensitive, you may be required to pack out ALL your human waste. This isn't as challenging as it seems. All you need to do is put a toilet seat over a waterproof container. You then make your deposit and close it up. You can then add the powdered product (mentioned in the previous section for wet garbage) that turns liquid waste into a gel and reduces odors.

Otherwise, you'll need to create your own natural bathroom. If you're just urinating, in most cases you'll want to find a spot far from the shoreline or any trails. On high volume rivers or in dry areas that see a lot of traffic, campers are sometimes advised to pee directly in the water. If you're doing more than just peeing, you'll need to dig a small hole (sometimes called a "cat hole") about 6 inches (about 15 cm) deep in the active layer of soil, at least 50 feet (or 20 meters) from the shoreline. Put together and pack a bathroom kit that is made up of a small trowel (for digging the hole), toilet paper kept in a plastic bag, some hand sanitizer, and a paper bag (lunch size, into which you'll put your used toilet paper) kept inside another plastic bag. This paper bag will then be burned on the fire at the very end of each day, or packed out with the rest of your garbage. This whole kit can be packed easily and discreetly in a small dry bag and shared in a small group. Either way, you'll want to bring enough paper bags so that you can use a new one each day. The problem with burying toilet paper is that it doesn't decompose quickly and often is dug up and scattered by animals.

In the far north, where the summer is short and the active layer of soil is thin and thawed out only briefly, it is recom-

ABOVE Although inappropriate in most areas, in the far north it is recommended to relieve oneself right on the ground... not to bury it.

mended that you defecate right on the ground, well above the high-water line of any rivers or lakes. If human waste is buried, it will take much longer to decompose than if it is left exposed.

In some coastal saltwater areas, the most responsible place to deposit human waste is in the inter-tidal zone, to make use of what is sometimes called the inter-tidal flush. There is such an enormous volume of water moving through with tides and tidal currents that this method is more environmentally responsible than using cat holes on shore. Just be sure to communicate with the group about where the bathroom zone will be, and make sure that it is well down the shore from the campsite and any cooking or swimming areas.

ANIMAL-PROOFING YOUR CAMPSITE When small animals like mice, whiskey jacks and raccoons get into your food and garbage they're a nuisance; but when large animals like bears show up at your campsite, they can be dangerous. Most wild animals naturally avoid humans. However, if a bear has learned to not fear people and that humans can be a source of food, its behavior can be unpredictable and it may even enter occupied campsites in search of food. In extreme cases, wildlife authorities will have to destroy the animal. You can help prevent this very unfortunate situation and improve your safety by keeping your campsite clean, dumping your gray water far from camp and keeping your food and garbage inaccessible.

At the end of each day, make sure all the food is packed up and that you don't have any food or scented things in your tent at night, including toothpaste and deodorant. For canoe and rafting trips, barrel packs are the best protection for food against bears. It is fine to leave food barrels in the kitchen area clamped shut but if you have food in dry bags, which leak odors more easily and are more easily chewed or carried away, hang them in a tree away from the tents and out of reach of bears. "Out of reach of bears" means at least 10 feet high and 5 feet out (about 3 meters high and 1.5 meters out) from the trunk of the tree. On sea kayaking trips, seal food and garbage in the hatch of a kayak. On hiking trips, put the food and garbage in a single pack and hang it in a tree. If there are no trees, place the pack far from camp so that if a bear does investigate it, the bear is unlikely to come in contact with people. For hiking in treeless areas, there are also special bear-proof canisters and tough bear-resistant bags that you can consider using. These should also be placed far from camp.

ENVIRONMENTAL CONCERNS It is

impossible to have no impact on the environments that we pass through, but we can minimize that impact. By managing our waste responsibly and thinking about our food and packaging choices, we can have a positive effect on the environment and the awareness of our traveling companions. As environmental awareness and education evolves, camping practices and the condition of outdoor recreation areas have actually improved despite heavier traffic, but it does remain an ongoing battle. Any contribution you make, including letters and donations to environmental groups, can make a difference to protecting the special places you enjoy.

RIGHT Keeping food out of reach of hungry bears means hanging it at least 10 feet high and 5 feet out.

MENU PLANNING

CHAPTER 3

ABOVE A meal on the hot rocks.

Your menu will function as a master plan for all the meals to be eaten in the course of your trip. Designing your menu is the most important part of your trip planning. This master plan will help you determine how much food to bring, how to pack it and what equipment you need. Laying out your food plan will also help you make sure that you have a good variety of foods, meet nutritional needs and that you don't leave anything critical behind.

To create a menu plan, we recommend that you make a list of all the breakfasts, lunches, snack, appetizers, dinners and desserts that you want to include on a master list, then organize them into particular days and swap things around as required.

There are a number of factors that will help determine which recipes to choose for a particular trip, which we outline for you in this chapter, step-by-step.

STEP 1: CONSIDERING TRIP DETAILS
It's easiest to start with the factors that pertain to the trip itself.

LENGTH OF TRIP The longer your trip is, the more important it is to make sure that your food will meet nutritional needs, offer some variety and will not get stale or spoil by the end of the trip.

LOCATION OF TRIP If your trip is in a remote area and you have to purchase your fresh ingredients in a small community, you will likely not be able to get specialized ingredients. If you are going on an arctic trip, you will want to plan hearty meals that will help sustain your group in a colder and possibly windier environment. Fresh food lasts a lot longer without spoiling in the north, so you can count on fresh fruit and vegetables weeks into your trip. If you are in a warmer climate, you will want to plan lighter meals and be aware that spoilage can occur much more quickly.

TYPE OF TRIP You will have a slightly different menu plan depending on whether you will be rafting, canoeing, sea kayaking or hiking. As a rule of thumb, you can bring the heaviest and bulkiest food on a rafting or canoeing trip, but you might choose to go a bit lighter if there are frequent and long portages. On a sea kayaking trip, you can take a little less, and the items need to be smaller to fit in the storage hatches. On a hiking trip, you'll want to bring nutritious food in its most compact and lightweight form possible, because it all must be carried on your back. We'll cover this in greater detail later in this chapter, under *Menu Considerations for Different Trips*.

TRIP PARTICIPANTS It's a good idea to find out early if there are any food allergies or sensitivities in your group. Some common problems include allergies to nuts, peanuts and shellfish, as well as lactose and gluten intolerances. People on certain medications cannot tolerate such things as grapefruit and broccoli. You may have a vegetarian or two on your trip. Menus do not usually have to be modified too much for lacto-ovo (milk- and egg-eating) vegetarians because you can prepare meat separately and simply add it on top for the omnivores. Vegans present more of a challenge, because many camp-cooking recipes include cheese and/or eggs. If you have children on your trip, you may want to tailor your menu plan to kid-friendly dishes with fewer exotic spices, and to include extra hot chocolate, marshmallows, peanut butter and popcorn.

Considering trip participants is also a good time to determine if you are going to be the sole food organizer, or if others want to be involved in planning and preparing the menus and meals for the trip. For longer trips and larger groups, food planning and preparation can be fairly time consuming, and it's great to be able to share the load with friends. As part of your trip planning, it's wise to meet and discuss food-related ideas, expectations, costs and responsibilities early on, and then keep communicating about these issues with regularity right up to the day you pack for the trip. Depending on levels of experience with camp cooking and the group dynamics, you can find a system that works for everyone. For example, your group might work entirely cooperatively, or one person might agree to be the main coordinator who holds the master lists and delegates tasks to prevent anything from being left behind.

Tips!

Depending on who you're camping with, it can work really well to divide the group into "food teams" of two or three people. These groups can then be responsible for an equal share of meals, organized by day. With a reasonable amount of communication, you can avoid overlap, excesses and shortfalls, and end up with terrific variety.

ABOVE Bagels are durable and can last up to a week in ideal conditions.

STEP 2: CONSIDERING TYPES OF FOOD

Once you've assessed what basic trip-related factors will affect your food choices, you can consider what kind of food will be best to bring based on things like how perishable it is, nutrition, flavor, and variety.

DURABILITY AND PERISHABILITY Fresh meat, fruit, vegetables and bread add variety, texture and taste to your menu but some of these foods will spoil or be crushed easily. There are many factors affecting how long perishable foods will last including how ripe the food is when packed, the temperature during the trip, how the food is packed, contact with moisture or air, and how sensitive the fresh food is to being crushed. Check food that can spoil periodically during the trip so you can use it before it goes bad and to prevent the spoilage from spreading.

On the subject of durability, try to minimize food that is overly bulky or easily crushed (like nacho chips) or have it early on the trip.

With so many variables it is difficult predict how long perishable food will last but here are some basic guidelines:

BREAD AND BAKED GOODS Light buns and sliced white flour bread should be used in the first few days. Whole wheat un-sliced loaves will last a little longer if they aren't crushed.

Because pita bread is flat and dry, you might expect it to keep well, but it has a lot of surface area exposed to the air, so don't count on it past four or five days. Dry whole wheat bagels and rye and pumpernickel un-sliced loaves may last up to a week in ideal conditions. Heavy and dry sourdough loaves may last a little longer. Rich whole grain delicatessen bread will keep up to two weeks. It may be dry by that point but it still tastes good. Tortilla shells are quite durable, easy to pack, and if properly stored will usually last for two to three weeks. Crackers will last up to two months. Remember, there is always the option of baking fresh bread on the trip.

VEGETABLES Lettuce, loose greens, tomatoes and cucumber are usually only good for the first day or two. Mushrooms and zucchini will last a little longer, but check them carefully for soft spots. Cherry tomatoes are more durable than full-sized ones, especially if packed carefully. Broccoli, cauliflower and eggplant are the next to go, along with celery, which gets limp and loses appeal. Red and green pepper may last a week under ideal conditions, but check them carefully, they spoil from the inside and it is best to use them before any soft patches appear. Carrots will perspire more than some veggies and will go off quickly if they're moist, but if you keep them dry they will last about three weeks. Cabbage, potatoes, squash and onions will last about a month. Fresh garlic will last several weeks if it is packed well and kept dry.

BELOW To bring fresh meat, freeze it ahead of time and then wrap it in newspaper to insulate it.

BELOW Cantaloupe will last for up to a week, but fresh eggs should be eaten very early.

FRUIT Soft-skinned fruit like strawberries and raspberries are hard to keep past the first night. Grapes, cherries and apricots may only last another day because they crush and bruise easily. Cantaloupe, melon and grapefruit will keep for up to a week in ideal conditions. Some oranges will last up to two weeks. Lemons and limes often last a little longer. Make the most of citrus fruits by using the zest or peel as well as the fruit. Some apples can last up to three weeks. Avocados, if packed carefully when they are still hard, can last for a week or two.

Tips!

Buy some fruits and vegetables that are not quite ripe so that they last longer and will have time to ripen over the course of the trip.

DAIRY Yogurt needs to be used within a day or so, unless you are traveling in a cooler area where it can last up to a week if sealed well. Ricotta and cottage cheese can last a week if kept in their sealed original container. Some soft cheeses may only last a few days. In warm weather even harder cheese will get greasy. Most dry hard cheeses will last two to three weeks in ideal conditions.

MEATS AND EGGS Fresh meat really shouldn't be allowed to reach room temperature for more than an hour or so unless it is in a marinade. Chicken and fish are particularly sensitive. To bring fresh meat, freeze it ahead of time, and then wrap it in newspaper to insulate it. Eat it early in the trip.

Cooked meats such as cold cuts and ham slices may keep a bit longer but be very careful with any meat you are suspicious of being past its prime because it can make you much more sick than eating spoiled vegetables or fruit. Dry and greasy smoke-cured meats like salami and pepperoni will last for weeks.

Eggs may last beyond the first breakfast but they are difficult to transport so use them up sooner rather than later.

Food Perishables Chart

EAT FIRST	MEDIUM-LASTING	LONGEST LASTING
Thin skinned vegetables (tomatoes, lettuce)	Medium skinned vegetables (peppers, zucchini, cucumber)	Root vegetables (potatoes, carrots, onions)
Delicate fruit (pears, strawberries, peaches)	Thinner skinned fruit (apples, mangoes)	Thick skinned fruit (citrus, pineapple)
Poultry, pork, fresh eggs	Beef, fish	Dried or cured meats (salami, dried bacon)
Milk, fresh cream	Soft cheeses (ricotta, cream cheese, yogurt)	Hard cheeses (parmesan, cheddar, swiss)
Regular bread (buns, sliced bread)	Specialty breads (bagels, pitas, flour tortillas)	Dense breads (pumpernickel, rye)

VARIETY AND FLAVORS Variety is important on a trip and helps to make meals the pleasantly anticipated events they should be. A good rule to follow is to make sure that there are no back-to-back repeats. For example, have a rice-based dinner one day, and a pasta-based dinner the next. Try to get a reasonable variety in ingredients. Different spicing or styles of cooking, like Italian, Mexican or Asian can make the same basic ingredients taste very different. Because it is easy to inadvertently repeat commonly used ingredients (like tomato sauce) for two or three suppers in a row, laying the recipes out in a menu plan makes it easier to avoid repetition.

TEXTURES AND COLORS There are other ways to enhance your outdoor meals beyond simply serving up good flavors. Different textures will make food more interesting and different colors will make food more visually appealing.

Try planning a variety of textures for each meal. For example, you might serve something that crunches, something chewy and something smooth. If you are having a "one pot" meal, it's easy to add different textures with the appetizers or dessert.

To add color, use vegetables like carrots and red peppers. Even the small touches like decorating a cake with M&M's will make a dessert more festive, allow you to be a little creative, and are so easy to do.

ABOVE Cake on the Mountain River in the Northwest Territories, Canada.

COOKING TIMES AND DIFFICULTY Plan easy-to-make, quickly prepared meals for the end of long or tough days, and quick but nutritious breakfasts for mornings when you'll want to make early starts from the campsite. You may want to plan more complicated meals for rest or layover days, when you will have more time to prepare them, but you'll probably want to make simpler appetizers and desserts when the main course is complicated. Remember that it is usually easy to switch meals around if your schedule changes while you're on a trip.

USE OF OVENS, POTS AND STOVES Some meals will require more pots than others, so make sure your pot set and the space on the firebox can accommodate your meal plan. If you're carrying two Dutch ovens, or a box or reflector oven, try to make optimal use of your oven capacity. For example, if you are making a baked dish like lasagna for dinner, you might as well bake something else for dessert or some bread for the next day's lunch at the same time. With the Outback Oven, you can only bake one pan at a time so plan your baked dishes accordingly.

If you're using stoves for cooking, you'll need to be a bit more careful about how many dishes you can cook at once, and how long they'll take to cook. Make sure you're carrying enough fuel for the amount of cooking and baking you'll do.

VEGETARIAN MEALS With most "tripping" meals, meat can be eliminated entirely or added after the vegetarians have filled their plates. Fresh meats do not keep very long anyway, so many of the dishes later in a trip tend to be semi-vegetarian anyway. It's quite easy to have the meat products on the side.

Non-meat alternatives like dried soy chunks, ground soy, and a similar product sometimes labeled with the appetizing moniker "texturized vegetable protein" or TVP, have a meat-like texture, are great sources of protein and go well in stews, chili or stir-fries. You can easily get enough protein and calories from nuts, cheese and legumes.

If a trip participant is vegan, it is more difficult to adjust menus and meals because eliminating meat, dairy and eggs is simply more of a challenge. In this case, use of grains, legumes and nuts in a creative and nutritious fashion is critical. Consult a vegan cookbook for recipe options, but you should also work with the vegan participant to coordinate meal plans, and possibly consider having them bring their own specialized foods.

SPECIAL MEALS OR EVENTS Just because you're on a trip doesn't mean you can't be festive. Plan special meals or dishes for birthdays, national holidays, the final supper of the trip or other "theme" nights. Most people will really enjoy the extra effort and creativity you put into these meals.

RIGHT Birthday party on the French River.

Tips!

You can make any dinner special by picking a few wild flowers for the center of the table and lighting some small candles. Any special touches you do will be magnified by your already beautiful surroundings and add to the pleasure of sharing a meal in the outdoors.

NUTRITION There are four main groups of foods: 1) grain products, 2) vegetables and fruit, 3) dairy products, and 4) meat and alternatives. Each group contains certain nutrients essential for good energy and health. For optimal nutrition, is important to have representation in each meal from each of the food groups. You need different amounts from each group and require the most from the grain products group, second most from vegetables and fruit, third most from milk products, and the least from meat and alternatives. The more active you are, and the colder the temperatures, the higher the number of servings you need from each food group to meet your energy and nutritional needs.

GRAINS AND GRAIN PRODUCTS This group is an important source of carbohydrates, fiber, iron, minerals and vitamins, which energize our bodies and minds, and keep our blood and digestive tracts healthy. Build meals around your favorite grain, pasta or rice. Choose whole grain products as much as possible for the fiber and iron that they provide. We like to use whole rolled oats to make porridge in the morning; it takes slightly longer to cook, but it is more nutritious and tastes great.

VEGETABLES AND FRUIT This group is rich in essential vitamins A, C and folic acid. They help our bodies use energy and fight infections, are important for growth and contribute to healthy skin, eyes and hair. Choose dark green, bright yellow or orange vegetables and fruit more often for the special nutrients that they offer. For example, an apple (or apple juice) contains trace amounts of folate, whereas an orange can meet approximately 50% of your folate requirements. On wilderness trips, it is important to choose vegetables and fruit that will keep well. Cabbage, carrots, onions and potatoes are very good and keep for a long time on a trip. It is also possible to get dehydrated and freeze-dried varieties. You can add dried broccoli, bell peppers and cauliflower to your spaghetti sauce to add a bit of a veggie boost. Don't forget dried fruit such as peaches, pears, apples and banana chips for a great trail snack.

DAIRY PRODUCTS This group is an important source of calcium, which makes strong bones and teeth. It also helps our muscles to function. We need to include two to four servings of milk products each day. On trips we can supplement our supply by adding skim milk powder to our hot cereals as they are cooking. Cheese keeps well, and can be added to many dishes.

BELOW Vegetarian Chili.

Dried cheddar powder and grated parmesan are available at most bulk food stores.

MEAT AND ALTERNATIVES This group primarily delivers protein and is essential to build and repair muscle tissue and maintain healthy blood. You should get two to three servings per day. Options include meats, eggs, legumes (beans and lentils), soy products, nuts and fish.

On a trip, fresh meats and fish generally must be eaten within 24 hours of departure to ensure freshness. However, you can dehydrate or buy dried beef, chicken and turkey chunks, which rehydrate quite well. It's also easy to add canned tuna, salmon and chicken to your meals. More options are discussed in the section about *Dehydrated Foods* in *Step 5* of this chapter.

For a vegetarian menu, a combination of whole grains with legumes creates a full protein. Soy-based products are also a great alternative to meat. They come dried, and either ground or in chunks. Once rehydrated, they can be used in most dishes as a replacement for meat.

OTHER FOODS Some foods don't fit into the four food groups and are classified as "other foods". This group includes foods that are mostly fats and oils (margarine, butter, oil), foods that are mostly sugar (jam, honey, maple syrup, sugar), high fat and/or high salt snack foods (potato chips, pretzels, pastry), beverages (wine, beer, spirits), as well as herbs, spices and condiments. These are often foods that should be consumed with a degree of moderation. When choosing foods in this "other" category, look for varieties that are low in trans fats, low in salt and low in sugar. There have been many new products developed in these categories to help us eat as healthily as possible. We encourage you to take advantage of these options.

RIGHT Apple crisp is a surprisingly simple dessert to make in a camp kitchen.

STEP 3: PLANNING THE MEALS This is
the best part of planning a trip. If you plan the meals carefully
you can impress your group with a gourmet experience they
will remember for a lifetime.

Here are some basic things to keep in mind when you're
choosing your recipes.

BREAKFASTS A simple and nutritious breakfast can
consist of just one dish. A big helping of oatmeal (or any other
cereal) with fruit, nuts, milk and sugar can keep people going
until lunch. However, when you're accommodating different
tastes and appetites within your group, you may wish to
include a second complementary dish. This can turn a hasty
breakfast on the run into a more social and relaxing event.
We always include fruit with breakfast whether it is fresh
and served separately or dried and added to cereal. Pancakes,
bacon, eggs and home fries are popular with many campers.
You'll want to plan quicker breakfasts for days that you'll need
to cover a lot of ground, and more leisurely breakfasts for days
that are not going to be as time-sensitive.

If you have a little extra time and want to go that extra mile
for your group, consider doing some breakfast baking. Muffin
mixes and biscuits are quick to put together and take only 15
minutes to bake. One of Black Feather's most popular breakfasts
is freshly baked cinnamon buns. The baked items can cook
while the cereal and fruit is being eaten, so with a little pre-
planning, it really doesn't have to take up very much extra time.

Remember to include morning beverages like coffee, tea or
hot chocolate, depending on what people in your group like,
or you may have a mutiny on your hands.

LUNCHES Lunch usually consists of some type of bread or
crackers plus any of a variety of things to go inside or on top:
peanut butter with honey or jam; cheese, salami, and dried
or canned meats; or rehydrated hummus and other spreads.
Cucumber can last a day or two and adds some crispiness
to sandwiches.

Cold lunches often make the most sense because they are often eaten in the middle of the day when you are on the move. Sometimes it is nice to have soup or hot drinks, especially if the day is damp or chilly, and these can be prepared quickly if your stove is easily accessible.

Crunchy vegetables can round out a lunch by adding variety and complete the meal nutritionally. Top your lunch off with fresh or dried fruit and a treat like chocolate or cookies.

SNACKS

Even with three square meals a day, you can expect stomachs to grumble mid-morning and in the afternoon on cold or active days. Having some snacks on hand will go a long way towards keeping everyone happy and enthusiastic. Some favorite snacks include energy bars, granola bars, fresh or dried fruit, nuts, chocolate, pepperoni sticks, hard candies and GORP. Although GORP stands for Good Old Raisins and Peanuts, feel free to add all kinds of other stuff to the mix. A well-known trick is to buy trail mix and then kick it up a notch by adding a chocolate candy like M&M's or Smarties.

DINNERS

Dinner is usually a relaxed social time, and you can expect that people will be ready for a hearty meal after a full day outdoors. Sometimes you'll want a simple and easy-to-prepare meal, while at other times, the meal can represent the whole evening's entertainment.

APPETIZERS However simple or complicated your dinner is to be, having appetizers is a great way to start. It will temporarily fill the hunger gap, raise spirits and encourage people to help prepare and cook the rest of the meal. Your appetizers can be as simple as a bag of nuts, carrot sticks, or cheese and crackers; or as classy as smoked salmon with capers, red onions and cream cheese on crackers.

SOUPS Soups are usually quick to prepare, take the edge off a hunger and cheer people up on a cold or long day. Soup mixes are compact and quick to prepare, making them ideal camp food. You might choose to skip this course on hot days but because they don't take up much space or weight, you might pack them for each dinner anyway. You can serve them as is, or add veggies such as onions, cabbage, beets, potatoes or fresh herbs for variety.

Tips!

If the day has been particularly cold or long and you can sense people need a boost when they get to camp, you can get water boiling on your stove quickly and make soup as the first order of kitchen business. Getting the fire going and making the rest of the meal will naturally follow, but having a cup of hot and tasty soup soon after arriving at camp will work miracles in re-energizing and lifting spirits.

BELOW Breakfast before a big day.

BELOW Sushi appetizers.

SALADS It is nice to have something fresh and crunchy every few nights. Lettuce will keep up to three or four days if it's kept cool and is packed carefully, and cabbage will keep all summer. You can spice your salad up by adding some carrots, walnuts, raisins, cheese or other veggies. You can bring bottled salad dressings, prepackaged mixes or separate containers of oil, balsamic vinegar and spices to make your own dressing.

MAIN DISHES The options for main courses are endless. Some of the easiest and tastiest main courses include stir-fries, pasta dishes, hot roll-ups and fish. An oven opens up countless more meal options including pot pies and baked lasagna. For the first few nights you have the most options because you can use fresh produce and meat. Meat will last until the second night if it starts frozen and is wrapped in several layers of newspaper and plastic. You'll want some sort of starch carbohydrate to go along with your meal such as rice, pasta, legumes, bread or a starchy vegetable. Vegetables can be added to the dish or served on the side. Many fresh vegetables will keep the duration of your trip or you can use dehydrated ones.

DESSERTS After an active day in the outdoors, you can expect people to appreciate and have more room for desserts than they might in their normal lives. Some of the best desserts are simple ones that offer campers something tasty to nibble on while hanging around the campfire. It can be as simple as fresh fruits with cheese, nuts and chocolate, or cookies. A little port or ice wine is also a nice finish to a meal. There are mixes for desserts that only require some energetic whisking to prepare, like mousse, puddings and custards. Popcorn and cereal squares are quick to prepare in a pan on the stove or fire. Many baked dessert ideas are available if you have an oven. Most take only 5 or 10 minutes to prepare, and then about 30 minutes to bake, requiring minimal attention while you eat your meal or relax around the fire.

BEVERAGES During the day, people will have different preferences for what they like to drink. Some will prefer straight water and others will want something flavorful made with juice crystals. Sport drinks are similar to juice crystals in that they deliver sweet calories, but they also contain salt to keep electrolyte levels stabilized because these are depleted when people exercise and perspire. Consider the activity level for the trip and decide what is appropriate to bring.

Depending on the tastes of the group, you might bring wine or other beverages to sip before, during and/or after dinner. Boxed wine is terrific for camping because you can simply pack the bag from inside the box and recycle the box. These wine bags and their pouring valves are usually quite durable, but should still be packed with care. If you decide to bring bottled wine or spirits, you can decant these into Nalgene containers to avoid bringing heavy and breakable glass bottles.

Tips!

If you pack a bag of white wine for a sea kayaking trip, store it close to the bottom of the boat so that when the time comes to pour it, it's already chilled!

There are also the after-dinner drinks like tea and coffee, which are usually preferred in their decaffeinated versions in the evening.

SMUG OVEN CAKE

There was a lot to learn early in my guiding career. Before the Dutch oven became the standard way to bake on Black Feather trips, we used a variety of other techniques and equipment. The most popular was the folding Camp Oven designed for use with Coleman stoves. We'd use these ovens over a firebox too, but it was sometimes difficult to control the heat this way. While the goal, of course, was to build even heat with a properly prepared bed of coals, every now and then you'd get a flare-up that would burn the outside of some unsuspecting cake or Logan Loaf, resulting in a gooey raw center encased in a hard carbon shell. The trick for preventing this unappetizing outcome was to place a heat diffuser of some sort in the bottom of the oven. To the experienced, this diffuser would be a pan of sand or water; to the uninitiated (namely me), this was a nice flat round river stone collected from the gravel bar. Feeling quite smug about coming up with such a clever innovation on my first Nahanni trip with Jim Risk, I confidently placed the stone in the bottom of the oven, closed the door and stood back, happily anticipating the moment that I would extract a perfectly baked cake. In a matter of moments, there was a loud crack, the oven leapt a foot in the air and the door blew off, and the area in front of the door (including my legs) was strafed with rock shrapnel. Thus I learned two lessons: 1) river rocks are porous and full of water that can heat up and blast the rock apart like a piece of popcorn, and 2) rock chip-encrusted cakes are a hard sell even to river-hungry campers. (Logan Loaf is a recipe included in this book.)

– Chris Pullen (Nahanni River, 1992, guiding with Jim Risk)

ABOVE Dishing out lasagna from the Dutch oven.

STEP 4: DETERMINING QUANTITIES

Once the overall menu is determined, you can figure out how much you need of each thing. If you use a spreadsheet program on a computer, recipes and quantities can be easily modified for future trips or different numbers of trip participants.

Too much food means extra weight to carry and more space to find in your packs. However, this problem is much easier to deal with than going hungry. There are many factors that will affect how much people will eat, and careful consideration of them will help you bring appropriate amounts. If you bring enough, you'll have the freedom to adjust quantities on-the-fly when you're on the trip. At first, cook the entire amount that was brought for each meal. After about two days, you'll get a sense of whether it is a "big eating" or "small eating" group, and

can adjust the amount that you cook accordingly. It is easier to cook 2½ cups of rice when you've packed 3 (leaving half a cup of uncooked rice leftover) than to make too much then have to burn the leftovers or pack it out. Another way you can adapt meals to appetites on the trip is to omit a side dish like soup or appetizers, or switch parts of different meals.

Tips!

If you're on a longer trip in a remote area, it's especially smart to bring a little extra food, even an emergency meal in case of delays or unforeseen circumstances. Things like rice and soup are ideal for this because they are not very heavy, bulky or expensive. On the Hood River in Nunavut, Canada, we were picked up by the float plane two days late because of inclement weather, but we got by on extra rice, soup and pancakes. Having extra food makes delays part of the adventure, instead of causing stress and discomfort.

ABOVE Camping in Killarney Provincial Park, Ontario.

The sample menus at the end of this section will give you a starting point for the quantities to plan on for an average group. If you make notes during your trip on the quantities that you've actually used, you'll have a reference point for your next trip.

TIMING As the trip progresses, appetites increase. This phenomenon occurs because metabolism increases as a result of activity, and because almost all food tastes better eaten outdoors.

ACTIVITY LEVEL Appetites will increase on days when you've been very active. Hiking days, long paddling days or strenuous portaging or whitewater will require more calories than a lazy day around the campsite.

TEMPERATURES People need to eat more in cold or wet weather, just to provide the fuel to keep bodies warm. You will eat less on hot days but will need to drink more water and probably use more drink crystals, for example. We tend to skip the hot soups and even some of the baked desserts on hot weather trips and try to pack lighter, fresher tasting items.

GENDER Overall, men tend to eat more than women. For all-male trips, slightly increase the amounts certain ingredients, especially pastas, rice, breads and cereals. However, some women can eat very heartily too, so it is critical not to shave things down too much on all-female trips.

Food Quantities Table

TYPE OF FOOD	QUANTITY PER PERSON
Rice and pastas	
Rice	1/2 cup (125 ml)
Spaghetti	1/3 lb or 5 oz (150 g)
Fusilli	1 cup (250 ml)
Macaroni	1 cup (250 ml)
Orzo	1/2 cup (125 ml)
Couscous	1/2 cup (125 ml)
Cereals	
Granola	1/2 cup (125 ml)
Oatmeal	1/2 cup (125 ml)
5-Grain	1/3 cup (80 ml)
Wheatlets	1/3 cup (80 ml)
Baking mixes	
Pancake mix	1/2 cup (125 ml)
Muffin mix	1/2 cup (125 ml)
Biscuit mix	1/2 cup (125 ml)
Other	
Mac'n Cheese Powder	1/3 cup (80 ml)

STEP 5: BUYING AND PREPARING FOOD BEFORE THE TRIP
Now that you've figured out what you'll eat and how much you need, it's time to get it all together. Here we've collated what we know about finding the food you'll need and some of the many options available to you.

How long this step takes and how much you spend will depend on your personal preferences, whether you want to get pre-prepared food or make things yourself, and the general availability of the items you want.

Tips!

If your group has divided up the food-buying and pre-trip food preparation responsibilities, make sure that everyone keeps receipts to make the final accounting and cost-sharing easier. If different people are responsible for different meals, make sure you discuss the shared items too. It's a good idea to agree what will be in the staples kit, for example, and decide who will be responsible for gathering it together. If you all communicate and coordinate effectively, you won't end up with an over-supply or under-supply of anything.

BASIC INGREDIENTS
While you can buy many things on your list at a regular grocery store, your local bulk food or health food store is usually the better place to buy things like: pasta, rice, flour, sugar, spices and cereal (such as granola, oats, cream of wheat, and five-grain porridge). You can also find trail mix, nuts, dried fruit, sweets, and some dried vegetables.

Buying supplies at bulk food stores offers several advantages over buying at a regular grocery store: you can bag the exact quantity that you need, excess packaging is greatly reduced or eliminated, and finally, it is usually your most economical option.

Tips!

Asian food shops are full of delicious foods that are perfect for making your trip menu more interesting. Vietnamese hot sauce, for example, is a favorite condiment on macaroni and cheese or scrambled eggs. You can also find things like Pad Thai sauce, versatile curry pastes, and lightweight, fast-cooking rice noodles and dried mango. As you get more confident with your camp cooking, try getting some coconut milk which comes in a variety of forms: canned, in a compressed block or even in powder form. The type of trip you are doing will dictate which form is best for you. Besides using coconut milk with curry pastes to make wonderful sauces for stir-fries, you can add coconut milk to rice while you are boiling it to give it a lovely aroma and flavor; and add it to peanut butter sauces or to rice pudding desserts. Spring roll wrappers are also great for trips and can be used to make all sorts of tasty surprises. Wrap up chopped vegetables for classic spring rolls, cheese and pepperoni for pizza rolls, or chocolate chip and marshmallow for desert rolls. All you have to do is stuff them with something tasty then fry them up for a delicious quick appetizer.

DEHYDRATED FOODS There is a huge range of dehydrated foods to bring on trips. Dehydrated foods retain most of the nutritional value of fresh foods, but are much reduced in weight and bulk. On longer trips, dehydrated food is essential. It is simply not possible to carry enough regular food for three weeks. More and more dried foods are available at your local grocer, bulk food store, or specialty food shops, and if you have a food dehydrator, you can easily make a lot of your own.

FRUITS AND VEGETABLES Fresh fruits and vegetables are delicious but most of them will last only a few days and they're generally bulkier and easily damaged. The dehydrated versions are a good solution. Many fruits and vegetables dehydrate beautifully and they pack and keep well. It is true that they do not taste exactly like their fresh equivalents, but they still pack a lot of flavor and nutrition.

For cooking, ten minutes of soaking in water rehydrates most dried fruits and vegetables. Dried mushrooms, peppers, broccoli work very well when reconstituted in stir-fries and sauces. If you are including dried vegetables in a sauce like spaghetti, you can reduce the consumption of fuel and the use of an extra pot by just throwing the dehydrated vegetables right into the sauce pot. Just add a bit more water to let it absorb as it is cooking. This method works well and means less cooking and clean-up. Similarly, while dehydrated fruit can be eaten dry, it can also be reconstituted in a pot of hot cereal if you just add a little extra water when you cook it.

RIGHT Rehydrating a pea, corn, and chicken mixture.

Rehydrated blueberries and raspberries really add a lot of flavor to pancakes and baked foods. Dried apples and apple-sauce can be reconstituted and prepared into a fantastic apple crisp, which makes a tasty dessert or breakfast. Fruit leather is a popular snack and comes (or can be made) in a huge variety of flavors. Sometimes we spread cream cheese or peanut butter (or both) on fruit leather, roll it and slice it into cookies.

SNACKS AND DIPS Hummus, carrot and bean dips rehydrate really well for a lunch spread or dip. Meat, chicken and fish jerky are delicious snacks and add a lot of taste to soups, stews and stir-fries. Most dehydrated food is more expensive than fresh, but if you get a dehydrator, you can make much of it yourself, save money and have more food choices.

At breakfast time, put a dip mix (like dried hummus) in a sealable container with some water, mix it up and close it tightly. By lunch time the dip will be fully rehydrated and ready to eat.

DO-IT-YOURSELF DEHYDRATING To dehydrate foods, you can use your home oven, but most people use a dehydrator because it's faster, dehydrates more evenly and is much more energy-efficient. The dehydrator is an apparatus that has a stacked series of shelves, with a heating mechanism and some-times a fan on the bottom. Each shelf is usually made of a mesh,

and has a vent in the middle to allow steam to escape. The best food dehydrators have an adjustable temperature control and good air flow. You can usually find a range to choose from at most hardware and department stores.

The great thing about a food dehydrator is its versatility. You can do things like make delicious beef jerky, dehydrate whole tins of tuna, prepare a wide range of vegetables to go into soups and stews on trips and make your own fruit leather with spectacular combinations of flavors. If you have kids or just love fruit leather, you might find yourself making your own fruit leather regularly, whether or not a trip is planned. Either way, a food dehydrator can be a great investment.

Choose perfectly ripe and perfect produce. Some things, such as cauliflower, carrots and broccoli must be "blanched" first, (lightly steamed or boiled), and then dehydrated. Most fruits and vegetables can just be sliced into thin strips and laid on the shelves. You can also dehydrate things like tomato paste and salsa. Generally, the higher the water content of an item, the more difficult it will be to dehydrate.

Homemade tomato-based sauces and chili dehydrate and reconstitute very well and make great quick meals, going from bag to boiling water to plate in under 20 minutes and providing excellent flavor and nutrition.

When you are dehydrating meat, use the same rule as for the fruit and vegetables and choose meats/fish that are totally

BELOW Dips are tasty, versatile, and quick to prepare.

BELOW Pears Helene is a simple and delicious camping dessert.

fresh and in perfect condition. Then, slice them very thinly and dehydrate according to the directions of the dehydrator.

Once you have dehydrated your food, store it in clean, airtight containers or bags and label them so you know what they are, how much they'll make when reconstituted, and what meals they're for. If you keep dehydrated food refrigerated until the time of your trip, it will even last longer.

Tips!

If you decide to dehydrate your own food, plan your menu well in advance because food dehydration takes time and commitment. The average drying job (for example, making banana chips) requires a night in the dehydrator, so dehydrating can take a significant amount of pre-trip time to get everything dried and packed away. If you are going on a trip with a group, divide up the drying tasks between a few people. Otherwise, you might find yourself slaving away into the wee hours of the morning in the week before the trip.

FREEZE-DRIED FOODS You can also purchase many commercially freeze-dried items at specialty stores. These are a little more expensive, but they are extremely lightweight and rehydrate into much larger portions with minimal effect on the original flavor. Freeze-dried foods you might find include blueberries, strawberries and raspberries; vegetables such as peas, corn, cauliflower, mushrooms and broccoli; and meats such as ground beef, chicken chunks and turkey chunks.

RIGHT Pre-packaged meals have really improved over the years and are great options for small groups, especially when keeping your pack weight down is a concern.

One of the more useful items is freeze-dried eggs. "Yuck!" you might say. But dried eggs are necessary for baking recipes that call for eggs. They are also quite delicious when cooked into breakfast dishes like French Toast, Breakfast Burritos or Frittata. The trick is not to use them alone, as basic scrambled eggs. For that, you need the real thing.

PRE-PACKAGED FOODS There are several excellent brands that offer entire pre-packaged meals for camping available at outdoor specialty shops. Generally you can count on the quantities and instructions to be appropriate for outdoor trips and the meals to be tasty and nutritious. There are main dishes, snacks, desserts and baking mixes available. Getting a selection of these meals can make things easier for your first camping experience. While this simplifies some of the planning, purchasing and packing, it also reduces your flexibility to tailor the quantities and ingredients to your group and tastes. These meals also cost more because you're paying for someone else to refine the recipe and pack the ingredients.

There are many pre-packaged items that you can pick up at your neighborhood grocery store that are great for wilderness cooking. You can get some excellent spice combinations, such as taco seasoning mix and pasta seasoning mixes. You can purchase main course items, such as scalloped potato mixes, pastas, sauces and rice meals. There are some great desserts, too. Black Feather often uses "no-bake" cheesecake mixes and mousse mixes which are easy to prepare and taste good, especially if you dress it up with additional ingredients such as fruit or chocolate. You can add a bit of flair by topping your dessert or hot chocolate with a dollop of "whipped topping" which is available in a dried form. Most grocery stores have specialized areas, where you can pick up items for Asian, Mexican or East Indian dishes. You can also usually find nutritious "energy bars" in most grocery stores (not to be confused with "candy bars", which give energy but little or no nutrition).

Be cautious though, just because it is on a store shelf doesn't mean it will taste good. It is best to experiment at home before committing a hungry group's appetite to too many pre-packaged meals.

STEP 6: FOLLOWING THE MENU (OR NOT) ON TRIP

Now that you've created the perfect menu, you will want to make a couple of copies and plasticize one so that it doesn't get wet. Keep the plasticized menu at the top of the wannigan, main food barrel, or pack, as long as it is in a known and consistent spot so it is easy for anyone to find at each meal. If you keep a second copy in your map case you'll be able to ruminate over the upcoming meal during the afternoon's paddling.

You don't need to feel obliged to follow the menu plan to the letter. Especially as you gain confidence in your outdoor cooking skills, we encourage you to think of your menu plan more as a jump-off point or framework within which there is lots of room for creativity and imagination. You can switch meals around depending on cooking times, weather or whim. Sometimes we'll steal an ingredient from another meal. Mark learned a lot about creative cooking from a friend with whom he'd done several long northern trips. Around mid-afternoon this friend would look at the menu and start negotiating about supper. The resulting meals would be reviewed and critiqued in detail in the group log book, and would typically bear no resemblance to the original menu. Now when Mark knows this fellow will be on a trip, he packs random ingredients just to see what this guy will come up with.

BELOW Following the menu... or not?

THE EXTRAS: TAKING IT UP A NOTCH

There are a few ways you can take good food and make it great.

SPICE KITS Your spice kit is like a "food repair kit" and is an essential tool for the outdoor gourmet chef. A good variety of spices will allow you to adjust each meal to the tastes of the participants on your trip, as well as giving you more room to be creative. Small containers filled with dried herbs and ground spices don't take a lot of room and are lightweight. Just make sure your containers are watertight so you don't end up with a sodden mass at the bottom of the jar.

The amount and selection of spices you bring will depend on the recipes you've chosen, but there are a few staples: salt, pepper, parsley, cinnamon, oregano, basil, ginger, curry, dry mustard, red pepper flakes, garlic and chili powder. There are two basic approaches to the packaging and use of spices for a trip. You can carry all your spices separately in one spice kit and measure and add them to each dish as you cook. This approach allows room for creativity and flexibility in altering your meals. The other approach is to measure, mix and pack the spices for each meal in a small bag that is packed with that meal, which may simplify preparation. For long trips you might opt for a combination: pack some key spices for certain meals, and also carry small quantities of a range of spices in a separate kit.

Fresh garlic will last a long time if packed well and kept dry, and it will add real punch and depth of flavor to most savory meals.

Tips!

It is always better to add just a little (or the recommended amount) of seasoning to a dish, let it simmer, and do a taste test before you add more. Remember, it is often difficult, if not impossible, to neutralize a spice once it's in. If some people prefer less seasoning, let them serve themselves first, then add extra spicing for the "hot mouths", or simply have extra spice on the side so that each person can tailor the meal to their tastes. For similar reasons it can be good to "under-salt" food, so that everyone can add exactly how much they like after the meal is served.

GARNISHES These special touches are usually simple compact additions that can add to the taste, texture and presentation of the meal. Fresh or dried herbs like parsley, basil and cilantro add flavor and color. Pickles, olives, capers and chili or jalapeño peppers are tangy additions to lunches, salads or main dishes. Use the zest or peel from lemon, limes and oranges in addition to using the fruit itself.

Seeds and nuts, plain or toasted, are great on their own as a snack but they can also dress up a dish as well as adding flavor and nutrition. As you prepare your food for the trip, think of where a few chopped almonds, cashews, peanuts, walnuts, pine nuts or sesame seeds might take a dish to the next level.

BELOW Small Nalgene bottles are great watertight containers for your spices.

BELOW It doesn't take much to liven up a dish when camping.

SAUCES Commercially prepared sauces such as Tabasco, Worcestershire sauce, soy sauce, horseradish, ketchup, prepared mustards, chili sauces and relishes all have their place as accompaniments to a meal.

Tubes of food are very popular in Europe. In specialty stores that feature European food products, you can often find tubes of hot mustards and flavorful pastes like garlic, tomato, pesto, caper, olive and chili. Until the seal is broken these tubes do not need to be refrigerated. They can then last for about a week after opening. If packaged properly and closed tightly after each use, these tubes can be brought along to add flavor and variety to lunch sandwiches and dinner sauces, to make quick and delicious marinades for fresh fish and meats, or to add some pizzazz to appetizers.

GOURMET FOODS A full day in the fresh air always whets the appetite and food always seems to taste better outside. On a trip, you have time to prepare your meals leisurely, instead of in the whirlwind of your normal existence. You can savor each mouthful while watching the sun set over the mountain peaks. So why not take some really, really good ingredients? A few special touches like real maple syrup, truffle oil, Swiss chocolate or gourmet cheeses can make a trip meal extra special. Head over to your favorite gourmet food store to see what is available.

BELOW Fresh crabcakes on a bed of sea asparagus.

A wilderness trip is also a good time to hit up Mom for treats. "You know how bad camp food is. We'll be starving, and we'll only survive if you make us those delicious orange rolls you do so well."

EDIBLE WILDS If you've got an interest in edible wild plants, camping trips can be a great time to develop or share your knowledge. Berries and nuts are plentiful in some areas and make a good snack or a tasty addition to desserts. There are many delicious wild mushrooms and other wild vegetables. Take a guidebook along and be sure to identify them properly. You can often find fresh sage on mountain slopes, wild ginger in shaded forests and many other herbs that will add spice to your meals. There are lots of edible plants that were traditional food sources, such as cattail roots and pollen. Some of it is quite tasty and occasional sampling can give you a different perspective on the land around you. We encourage you to learn as much as you can about edible wilds.

Important Safety Tip

In addition to edible plants, there are some very poisonous ones, so be very sure you know what you've got before you start eating wild plants, mushrooms and berries. Other edible wilds must be ingested with caution or at the right stage of maturity. For example, wild peas are delicious and normally very safe to eat, but eaten in large quantities can lead to paralysis!

BELOW Fresh-picked wild strawberries!

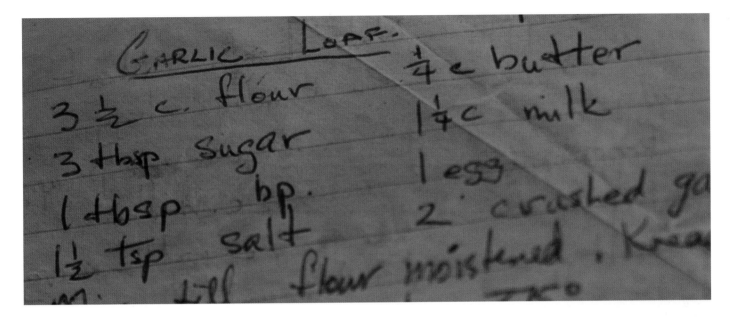

MENU CONSIDERATIONS FOR DIFFERENT TRIPS

Your menu plan will change depending on whether you are rafting, canoeing, sea kayaking or hiking. The main determining factors are space and weight.

RAFTING CONSIDERATIONS

On rafting trips, you have the luxury of the most space, the largest containers to carry the food in and the ability to bring the most weight. If you're on a rafting trip or a raft-supported canoe or kayak trip, you've likely chosen a river without many portages. Rafts can take bulky items and insulated coolers which will allow you to keep fresh food longer.

CANOEING CONSIDERATIONS

Canoes also have the capacity to carry a great deal of weight and bulk. However, even on a canoe trip, this can vary. If your trip is in an area like Algonquin or Quetico Park in Ontario, and you have chosen a route with countless portages, you will want to design a menu that is a bit lighter. On a river like the Nahanni in the North-west Territories, where there is only one portage, you can basically take everything and the kitchen sink... if you can fit it into your canoe!

SEA KAYAKING CONSIDERATIONS

On sea kayaking trips, the weight is not that much of a factor because you usually won't be portaging, so the limiting factor is space. Your food must be packed into smaller bags and containers, so that it can fit into the bow and stern hatches of the kayaks, some of which are only seven inches (17 cm) in diameter. Most kayaks have less carrying capacity than a canoe; the volume per person is proportionally smaller.

HIKING CONSIDERATIONS

Hikers have to carry all of their food and equipment, so when you're planning your menu you must constantly consider weight and bulk. Because you are expending energy to carry every ounce of food that is in your pack, you don't want to be carrying empty calories. A hiking menu needs to be tasty, compact, light and nutritious. Hiking menus usually include a lot of dehydrated food.

MENU EXAMPLE To help get you started, we've provided an example menu and staples list for a four-day hiking trip for six people. Quantities in the menu are approximate and provided just to demonstrate how you might work out required amounts when you're planning a menu.

FOUR-DAY HIKING TRIP - SAMPLE MENU
The following is a sample menu for a four-day hiking trip for six people. Quantities are approximate. Note that in a hiking-oriented menu, most of the food should be dried to save weight.

Menu Chart 1 of 2

	DAY 1	DAY 2	DAY 3	DAY 4
BREAFAST		2 cups (500 ml) yogurt 3 cups (750 ml) dried berries 3 cups (750 ml) granola **Egg Frittata** 6 English muffins	2 cups (500 ml) quick oats 3 cups (750 ml) dried fruit brown sugar cinnamon milk powder	3 cups (750 ml) granola 1 package dried apple sauce 3 cups (750 ml) muffin mix
LUNCH	6 whole wheat buns 9 oz (250 g) cold cuts 2 tomatoes lettuce 11-14 oz (300-400 g) sliced cheese 6 granola bars 6 apples	6 bagels 2 x 9 oz (250 g) cream cheese 1 tube olive paste 1 package alfalfa sprouts 1 bag fig newtons	1 loaf dense rye bread 11-14 oz. (300-400 g) cold cuts 11-14 oz. (300-400 g) cheese 6 power bars	2 pkg dense whole-grain crackers 11-14 oz (300-400 g) cheese 1 package dried hummus olive oil garlic 6 granola bars

	DAY 1	DAY 2	DAY 3	DAY 4
APPETIZERS	1 package rice crackers 1 brie 1 tin smoked oysters	1 package crackers 1/2 lb (250 g) cheddar cheese red & green grapes	fruit leather	2 cups (500 ml) mixed nuts
DINNER	**Pesto-Pine nut Pasta** spiral noodles 1 onion, garlic 1/2 dried broccoli, cauliflower 1 dried green pepper 1 dried red pepper 10 dried mushrooms dried pesto mix 1 cup (250 ml) pine nuts 1 cup (250 ml) parmesan cheese **Salad** lettuce, tomato, cucumber, feta **Vanilla Pudding with Brandy**	**Chicken Stir-Fry** 3 cups rice (750 ml) uncooked 4 boneless chicken breasts, dried or fresh; or 1 cup (250 ml) firm tofu 1 onion 2 garlic ginger 1 dried zucchini 1/2 dried broccoli, cauliflower 1 dried green pepper 1 dried red pepper 10 dried mushrooms 2 dried carrots almonds, cashews, sesame seeds **Pears Helene**	**Spaghetti** Whole wheat spaghetti noodles 2 packages dried parma-rosa sauce 2 cups (500 ml) sundried tomatoes 1 cup dried mushrooms 1 onion fresh garlic 2 cups parmesan **Chocolate Mousse** **1/2 cup popcorn**	**Burritos** 12 large whole wheat tortillas 2 packages dried refried beans 1 can tomato paste, dried 1 cup (250 ml) each dried mushrooms, peppers 1 pkg taco spices 9 oz (250 g) cheddar, grated 3 cups (750 ml) white basmati **Unbaked Chocolate Drop Cookies**

FOUR-DAY HIKING TRIP - STAPLES The

following is a list of basic staples for a four-day hiking trip for six people – not including the ingredients required specifically for your menu.

Four-day Hike

BASIC STAPLES

peanut butter	1 cup (250 ml)
jam	1 cup (250 ml)
honey	½ cup (125 ml)
margarine or butter	½ cup (125 ml)
oil	1 cup (250 ml)
brown sugar	½ cup (125 ml)
milk powder	3 cups (750 ml)
hot chocolate powder	1 ½ cups (375 ml)
coffee	½ lb (1/4 kg)
tea	12 bags
herbal tea	12 bags
juice crystals	1 package
soup	6 packages (3 each night)
soy sauce	¼ cup (60 ml)
GORP/trail mix	1 bag per person
toilet paper	3 rolls
dish soap	½ cup (125 ml)
bleach	1 tbsp (15 ml)
hand soap	1 bar
dish cloths	1
quick-dry all-purpose cloth	1
pot scrubber	1
dish towels	1
garbage bags	1

Spices:

salt	ginger
pepper	cinnamon
chili powder	oregano
basil	garlic

PACKING THE FOOD

CHAPTER 4

After you've completed planning your menu and you're finished any shopping or dehydrating that was required, it's time to pack. Packing has the following goals:

- to organize the food that you have by meal and by day, so that it is easy to access when you are on the trip

- to waterproof the food, in case of wet weather, or in case your boat capsizes if you are kayaking, canoeing or rafting

- to eliminate (and recycle when possible) any bulky packaging that the food originally came in

Everything except fresh food can be purchased and packed ahead of time. Fresh foods should be purchased as close to the trip as possible so they will last longer, but they will also require some preparation and packing.

Leave enough time so that you won't be rushed. If you're organized, you can shop and pack the food for a weekend trip in a half a day, while a two-week trip might take three full days. It can be much more enjoyable to spread the packing out over the week prior to the trip. There may be some last minute adjustments in your menu if you get inspired while shopping or if some of the ingredients you'd planned on aren't available. If you have time you can try several grocery stores, delicatessens, specialty food shops and outdoor stores to get exactly what you want and in the best condition.

LEFT For canoeing and rafting trips, the barrel pack is ideal for packing food.

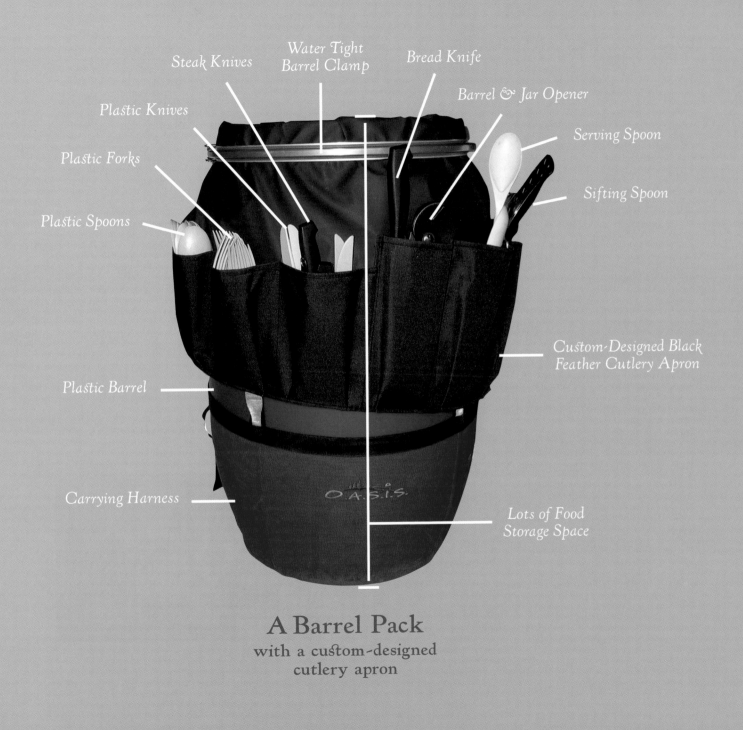

Steak Knives

Plastic Knives

Plastic Forks

Plastic Spoons

Water Tight
Barrel Clamp

Bread Knife

Barrel & Jar Opener

Serving Spoon

Sifting Spoon

Custom-Designed Black
Feather Cutlery Apron

Plastic Barrel

Carrying Harness

O.A.S.I.S.

Lots of Food
Storage Space

A Barrel Pack
with a custom-designed
cutlery apron

ORGANIZING AND WATER-PROOFING FOOD

If your food is organized and waterproofed, you eliminate most reasons to worry about it on the trip. When it is organized, you can always find what you are looking for, you will always have enough, and you will always have all the ingredients you need. When it is waterproofed, rain and even accidentally immersing your food packs will cause no undue stress about whether or not your supplies survived.

PLASTIC BAGS Plastic bags are used to repack items into meal-sized portions. Black Feather uses a number of different types of bags, in a variety of thicknesses rated by weight capacity. You can find these specialty plastic bags at a specialty plastics retailer. Check your yellow pages for outlets in your area. The bags we use range from 1 lb (the smallest) to 50 lb bags (quite large). We use smaller bags for packing spices and additions to dishes (such as nuts and raisins). We use medium size bags (5, 8 or 10 lb bags) for packing things like rolled oats, noodles and rice. We use the larger bags (25 and 50 lb) for packing meals (a complete breakfast might fit into a 25 lb bag and a full day's worth of dried food fits into a 50 lb bag). Bags also come in different thicknesses. Generally speaking, the larger the bag, the thicker the plastic needs to be. Some smaller bags have thicker plastic, and these are great for packing items like spaghetti noodles, which have a nasty habit of puncturing thin plastic bags.

If you don't want to go to the trouble of getting specialty plastic bags, you can use zip-lock or slide-lock bags. The "freezer" zip-lock bags are generally better because they are made of thicker and more durable plastic; and the ones that allow a full seal are better than the ones that have a zipper-type piece that you pull across, because this type often leaves a tiny hole unsealed at the end. Be cautious with zip-lock bags in general. They certainly have a place in your food packing, but it is not easy to guarantee that they will be waterproof, particularly over time. The closure mechanism must be kept clean to get the best seal, and undue stress should not be put on the bags or the closure. Double-bag things that would be a real mess if they leaked, or put things that absolutely must not spill into plastic bottles that can be reliably sealed.

Tips!

Live and learn, right? Although it may seem excessive to double-bag everything or bring only tested leak-proof containers, imagine a spilled container of garlic salt in your main food barrel. Trust me, there is nothing worse then 21 days of garlic-salt flavored everything.

GLASS BOTTLES Some foods like salsa, olives or Tabasco come in a perfect "trip-sized" container, except they're often made of glass. Leaving these things in their original bottles and jars is convenient as long as they don't break. Some parks restrict you from carrying glass to reduce the chance of broken shards being left behind by inconsiderate campers. If you have a choice, you can decant the contents into a plastic container, or take the glass bottle if you're careful packing them and clean up thoroughly if you break them. To minimize the chance of breakage, you can tape a layer of newspaper or plastic around glass containers. Even wrapping a few rounds of duct tape around will reduce the incidence of fracture.

BELOW Carefully packed food.

PLASTIC BOTTLES There are many commercially available plastic or Lexan containers on the market, which are great to store liquids and other foods for your trip. The most popular and waterproof are Nalgene containers. These come in a variety of sizes, in hard and soft plastics, with a variety of opening sizes. The harder plastic containers tend not to absorb flavors as much as the softer plastics. Black Feather uses "small mouth" Nalgene bottles for liquids like cooking oil, vinegar, lemon juice, maple syrup, and soy sauce, and "wide mouth" Nalgene bottles for foods like coffee, hot chocolate and milk powder. There are also straight-sided Nalgene jars that are perfect for peanut butter, jam, honey and margarine. These containers can be washed out and re-used trip after trip for an added economical bonus.

There are all kinds of food-grade plastic bottles that can be used to decant your foods, but remember that there are few things worse than finding that your bottle of olive oil or maple syrup has just leaked all over your sleeping bag! If you are unsure of how leak-proof a specific bottle might be, do a few tests prior to the trip. Put the food in the bottle, screw the top on securely and then perform the following test: tip it upside down and swirl it around, then put it on its side and put some pressure on the sides, and finally shake and jostle it around, as it might be in the field. If you are totally satisfied that it won't leak, then take it on your trip.

DRIED FOODS Each ingredient for each meal will get double-bagged in thick plastic. First, take the food out of the original wrapping and recycle it if possible. If there are directions on the box, you can cut them out and set them aside. Put the food in the inner bag and suck or press any excess air out to minimize space and prevent punctures. (You can't puncture a deflated balloon, but it's easy to pop an inflated one!) Use a permanent marker to write what the food is, as well as the meal and day it is destined for. (This stops you from mistaking the Day 5 breakfast pancake mix with the parmesan cheese for the Day 3 dinner.) Tie the first bag closed and put it in the second bag with the cooking directions. Tie the second bag closed separately. Close bags with a twist tie (but be careful that the ends of the twist tie cannot puncture the bag) or by tying a knot in the bag. With this system, water has to go through two sets of knots before reaching your food.

If you are taking cans, label the top of the can with a permanent marker. It's easy for labels to come off on a trip, leaving you to wonder if this is canned fruit for the Day 6 breakfast or tomato sauce for the Day 2 supper. Cans do not have to be bagged, but make sure that they are in the same barrel/pack/kayak as the rest of the dried food for that day.

Once you have double-bagged each ingredient for each meal, lay the food out by the meal and day on a table, shelves or on the floor. This gives you another visual check to see that you

THE MENU ACCORDING TO JIM

Black Feather trip food is carefully packed using a system of day bags, with each bag containing exactly (and only) what you need for each day's meals. As a Certified Control Freak, this system works well for me and ensures that through the whole trip every meal comes off pretty much exactly as planned.

(ON MY FIRST TRIP WITH JIM RISK, WHO HAS A MORE LAISSEZ-FAIRE GUIDING STYLE THAN ME, HE SUGGESTED THAT THE FOOD WOULD FIT MORE COMPACTLY IN THE BARRELS IF WE DUMPED THE FOOD OUT OF THE DAY BAGS AND PACKED THEM LOOSE INTO THE BARRELS. JIM IS VERY PERSUASIVE AND SO AGAINST MY BETTER INSTINCTS, I WENT WITH IT. EVERYTHING WORKED WELL FOR THE FIRST WEEK OF THE TRIP. WE WOULD CRACK OPEN A BARREL, DIG THROUGH FOR INGREDIENTS, AND MAKE EXCELLENT MEALS WITH WHAT SEEMED LIKE A LIMITLESS SELECTION OF FARE. TROUBLES STARTED LATER IN THE TRIP WHERE BY DAY 14 OR SO, HAVING PILLAGED ALL THE MORE INTERESTING INGREDIENTS EARLIER ON IN THE TRIP, WE WERE DOWN TO CREATIVE COOKING WITH A FEW BAGS OF WHITE RICE, WATER CHESTNUTS, TOMATO PASTE, BLACK OLIVES, AND A SELECTION OF MISCELLANEOUS BAGS OF WHITISH POWDER WITH LONG-FADED LABELS – ANYTHING FROM PANCAKE MIX TO PLAIN FLOUR. AND SO, BLACK FEATHER WITNESSED THE BIRTH OF THE LESS-THAN-EXQUISITE FRIED RICE ON A BED OF PANCAKES WITH TOMATO DIPPING SAUCE ON THE SIDE (YOU WILL NOT FIND THESE RECIPES IN THIS BOOK). THANK GOODNESS WE STILL HAD WINE IN THE STASH. I HAVE STUCK WITH THE DAY BAG SYSTEM EVER SINCE.)

– Carolyn Pullen, (Mountain River, 1990, guiding with Jim Risk)

have the right quantity and all the components for each meal.

The next step is to use a larger bag and put all of the items for this meal in that bag. In this way, you have everything dried that you need for breakfast on Day 4 in one bag. This bag might be a stuff sack, dry bag or a larger sized plastic bag. Finally, consolidate all of the meals (breakfast, lunch, dinner) for Day 4 into one "day bag". This is a larger bag (we get special thick plastic bags called 50 lb bags from a plastic retailer) that will fit all of these meals. This method is particularly good for canoe trips, where you have space for larger items in your pack. This takes a little more space in the barrel pack or dry bag but it reduces the chance of forgetting or losing something like the parmesan cheese for the pasta sauce.

FRESH FOOD For short trips, it can be a good idea to pack the fresh food with each meal that it is meant to go with. For longer trips, it is usually better to keep all the fresh food together so it is easier to monitor its condition, which will help ensure that you'll have enough to last the trip. Put fresh foods together into logical groupings:

- **vegetables and fruit**
- **meat and dairy**
- **breads**

Double-bag all of the breads ahead of time, making sure to eliminate excess air from the bags. Freeze your meats ahead of time and then wrap them in newspaper for insulation.

Tips!

If you're going to bring any baked goods with you on your trip, here's a great way to minimize how crushed they get. Collect empty cereal boxes and clean cardboard milk cartons for packaging - they have a waxy interior that is great for protecting food. Once your baking has cooled, wrap it in plastic food wrap and then tinfoil. Then, cut open your cereal box or milk carton to use as the final layer. Secure the whole thing with packing tape. The cardboard can be burned in the fire when you're done with it.

For fruit and vegetables, bag each variety separately. If you have time to cut off things like cauliflower stalks and husk your corn ahead of time, this will save space and cut down on the amount of garbage that you have to deal with. Some vegetables store better in a dry state. You can use paper towel to wrap things like mushrooms, peppers, garlic and onions, which will increase their life expectancy on the trail. If you wash and dry vegetables that will be eaten raw, you won't have to worry about using up treated water to wash them on the trip.

Tips!

Greasy, slippery, sweaty cheese is not very appetizing. Fortunately there is a trick for keeping your cheese structurally intact on summer trips. Dip a clean, new cheese cloth or dish-washing cloth (like a J-cloth) in a bowl of white vinegar. Wring out the cloth as much as possible, and then wrap a block of cheese in it. Wrap the cheese and cloth with plastic food wrap and then double-bag it. When you unwrap the cheese once you're out on your trip, you might notice slight discoloration or a faint taste of vinegar but at least it won't be a slippery mess!

STAPLES Staples are the things that you use for almost every meal, every day. These include peanut butter, jam, honey, margarine, salad dressing, brown sugar, tea, coffee, hot chocolate, milk powder, cooking oil, olive oil, vinegar, white flour, corn starch (for thickening sauces), mustard and spices. We also recommend including matches, lighters, dishwashing soap, dishcloth, tea towels and a scrubby in your staples list so they don't get forgotten. These need to get packed ahead of time.

For staples, we recommend using plastic screw top containers like Nalgenes, discussed above in the section on *Plastic Bottles*. For the dry items like brown sugar and coffee, you can also use plastic bags and twist ties or knots, or zip-lock bags to save space and expense. However, for repeated use, the plastic screw top containers are more durable and much easier to use.

If you have more of one staple food than fits in the available Nalgene container, put the extra amount in a plastic bag and refill the container when it's empty. You can even use thick, well-sealed plastic bags for extra peanut butter, honey and jam, but you'll want to triple-bag to avoid a mess. When a container needs refilling, you can simply snip one corner off with a knife, and squeeze the extra food into the Nalgene.

BELOW It's a good idea to keep all your staples together.

EQUIPMENT FOR PACKING AND CARRYING FOOD

BARREL PACKS The barrel pack is ideal for carrying food and equipment on a rafting or canoe trip. It is a 10 to 15 gallon (30 to 60 liter) plastic barrel that has a metal clamp and gasket that secures a plastic lid on top and creates a waterproof seal. Most outdoor stores sell them with a harness system that makes them easy to carry. The great thing about barrel packs is that they are easy to load, comfortable to carry and they last forever. This makes them ideal packs for personal equipment, although they are particularly useful for carrying food. They protect the contents from bruising and are also fairly smell-proof and secure against critters. I have even seen a barrel that a curious black bear unsuccessfully tried to investigate. There were claw and teeth marks all over the barrel but no perforations. They are a bit heavy and small for use on hiking trips and won't fit in a sea kayak.

COOLERS Small coolers will help fresh food last longer even if you don't take ice or ice packs in them. They are really only suitable for raft trips and some canoe trips. They can be strapped and carried like the traditional wannigan (see below) or if you're not doing much portaging, you can just carry them by the handles. In any case, make sure that the cooler has a secure closure, preferably a strap system that is separate from the latch installed by the manufacturer. If you capsize, you don't want the cooler to open and let your fresh produce float away. In rafts, large coolers can replace the inflatable thwarts or seat on the rowing rigs.

CANOE PACKS A canoe pack is a large nylon or (traditionally) canvas pack that doesn't have a frame, but has shoulder straps and a capacity of 20 to 30 gallons (80 to 120 liters). They are the largest of your carrying options and the easiest to pack, but they are not waterproof, and are not crush resistant. This means that you'll need to use several smaller dry bags inside the canoe pack. You will also want to insure that any food items carried in a canoe pack are well waterproofed and are not going to be damaged if somebody inadvertently sits on it. To make carrying them easier, canoe packs sometimes have a tumpline in addition to shoulder straps. The tumpline goes across your forehead and takes some of the weight off the shoulder straps. When the tumpline is adjusted properly it is quite comfortable but doesn't allow you to move with head and neck.

INTERNAL FRAME HIKING PACKS An internal frame pack is very similar to the canoe pack, but it is usually slightly smaller and has a more comfortable harness system with a hip belt. Internal frame packs have the most comfortable system for carrying heavy loads over long distances.

Internal frame packs with 60 to 90 liters of carrying capacity are the most efficient for carrying. They are recommended for hiking trips and can be used with dry bags inside for rafting and canoe trips. A well-padded hip belt and internal stays distribute the weight between your hips and shoulders. Look for good ventilation on your back and adjustments to keep the load closer to your body when you need more stability. Get a pack that fits your torso and learn to adjust it to fit your body.

The fabric will often have a waterproof coating but the seams, zippers and openings are not usually waterproof. Still, they are usually enough to keep the contents dry in all but heavy, sustained rain. In such cases, you can use a waterproof pack cover that works like a shower cap to cover the pack. The pack cover is usually adequate for hiking trips, but if you are doing a lot of stream crossings where your pack has the potential to be accidentally immersed, you may want to put at least your essential equipment and food in dry bags inside the pack. Electronics and critical equipment should certainly be in waterproof dry bags or containers. If you are canoeing or rafting, all your water-sensitive equipment and food should be in dry bags.

DRY BAGS Dry bags are reliable and functional options for waterproofing equipment and they come in a huge variety of sizes and styles. You can get them small enough for carrying a snack, or you can get them as large as a barrel pack with straps

ABOVE A dry pack is a dry bag that can be worn like a backpack. The only downside is that they don't protect food as well as a barrel does.

and a harness. Small ones can be stuffed inside internal frame and canoe packs. Some dry bags have extra features like clear panels that allow you to see what's inside, or a purge valve to remove excess air.

Dry bags made from PVC material are tough and inexpensive but heavy. They are also much more difficult to slide past each other, particularly when stuffing them into the hatches of a sea kayak or into a pack. Also note that PVC is environmentally unfriendly and potentially hazardous to your health. Urethane-coated nylon is lighter and the slippery outer surface is easier to pack because it slides into a pack or sea kayak compartment more easily. They are a little more expensive, so whether you choose nylon, PVC, or a combination will depend on the types of trips you plan on doing.

Tips!

The key to keeping a dry bag waterproof is to close it correctly. If you are using a roll-down model, make sure that you flatten the opening, fold it over several times, and secure the ends. Some bags come with a defined guideline for how many folds are required to guarantee that they will be waterproof.

DRY PACKS These are similar to smaller dry bags but include shoulder straps and sometimes a hip belt for carrying. All of the seams are welded and waterproof but because of the larger opening great care must be taken in closing them to ensure a watertight seal. They are not as reliably waterproof as a barrel or smaller dry bags.

WANNIGAN For the kitchen equipment, you might consider using a wannigan. A wannigan is a large box made from thin plywood or plastic and is used to carry the pots and kitchen equipment. Some have a gasket to help keep the contents dry.

The advantage of the wannigan is that it makes it easy to organize the kitchen equipment and at camp it provides a nice flat area to sit on or play chess and checkers. The disadvantage is clear when you try to carry one. They are best carried using only a tumpline attached close to, or at the top of the box and the loop should extend about 12 to 16 inches (30 to 40

centimeters) beyond the attachment points. When you are carrying it, lean forward and distribute the weight between your straight spine (via the tumpline) and your shoulders (with the box resting on your shoulder blades). You need a particular personality to successfully carry a wannigan. This personality ideally comes with a stocky body, no neck and a hunger for punishment.

There are also mini-wannigans available, which are perfect for carrying the staples on a canoe trip. They hold, almost perfectly, the containers for your peanut butter, jam, honey, margarine, etc, and make them very easy to organize. You can bring the mini-wannigan out at every meal.

BELOW Dry bags with clear panels are really handy for keeping track of food on camping trips if several bags are being used.

BELOW The wannigan is really convenient for carrying all your kitchen equipment, but it isn't the easiest thing to portage.

ABOVE Canoeing in Algonquin Park, Canada.

PACKING CONSIDERATIONS FOR DIFFERENT TRIPS
The way you pack your food will also depend on what kind of trip it is; rafts, canoes, kayaks and hiking packs are very different vessels. The one principle that applies to packing for all these trips, however, is that it's important to organize your food so that it is easy to get at and logically arranged. If things are packed randomly you'll spend all your time at camp looking for your ingredients instead of enjoying the much more pleasurable activities of cooking and eating. Here are our packing tips for each type of trip.

Because the way you'd pack for canoeing and rafting trips is very similar, we've grouped those together.

CANOEING AND RAFTING CONSIDERATIONS
On canoeing and rafting trips, you'll use packs, coolers, barrel packs, a wannigan, or a combination of these.

SHORT TRIPS To pack for shorter trips (two to four or five days), start with the last day's food at the bottom of the pack or barrel and work your way up. If you pack carefully, you can maximize the space you have and still keep hard things like cans away from crushable things like crackers. It will be easiest once you're out there if all the ingredients for a meal or even all the food for a complete day are packed in a larger plastic bag within the barrel or pack. Then you just have one bag to grab and are left with a sturdy bag for garbage in the evening when it is empty. This packing method takes up a bit more space, but it keeps things well organized. Another way to do it for short trips is to pack three separate breakfast, lunch and dinner bags, and again, start with the last day's food at the bottom.

LONG TRIPS On longer trips, Black Feather uses a system of barrels for dry food (Days 1 to 4, Days 5 to 7, Days 8 to 10) which are labeled and assigned to specific canoes. We also have a fresh produce barrel, and a deli barrel (breads, meat and cheese) and a staples barrel or wannigan. Depending on the size of your group, this many barrels might not be necessary, but dividing

the types of food this way is a good idea. If you store all your staples together in a separate container, it makes these common ingredients easy to access for each meal.

A barrel pack is particularly useful for produce, because it helps prevent crushing and bruising, which causes faster spoilage. Pack more durable items (onions, carrots, cabbage) towards the bottom of the barrel and softer items (tomatoes, mushrooms, fruit) at the top.

If you are on a warm-weather trip, line your fresh produce barrel and make an inner lid with cardboard or foam to insulate the barrel and keep things cool longer. Wrap frozen meats or fish in a few sheets of newspaper to insulate them. Remember that fruits and vegetables will get wet with condensation. Check

them periodically and dry them off to prevent early spoilage. Get rid of (or cut the bad parts off and eat the rest of) anything that is starting to spoil, because otherwise the spoilage can spread.

At camp, store the fresh food barrel or cooler in a shady area, or even in cold water. Hot temperatures will increase spoilage, and having a barrel sit in the sun for a few hours turns it into an oven.

SEA KAYAKING CONSIDERATIONS Packing a
sea kayak is an art, but you can get a lot in there if you maximize your use of those narrow spaces in the hull. Because you have to maneuver everything through the hatches and because keeping food completely dry is imperative, a lot of your food is

ABOVE Hiking in Canada's far north.

best packed in dry bags, most of it in 1.5 to 3 gallon (about 5 and 10 liter) sizes. Nylon dry bags cost a little more than PVC dry bags but when you are trying to stuff bags alongside each other into the hull, you will appreciate how much more easily nylon bags slide past each other; PVC dry bags tend to stick to each other. You can use a combination of types, since nylon bags will also slide easily past PVC bags. Just be sure to balance the weight evenly between bow and stern so you won't affect the "trim" or performance of the craft.

It makes sense to put items for the last days of your trip far into the bow or stern so you won't have to keep repacking in the first days. Most sea kayaks have a larger compartment with a bigger hatch in the stern and a smaller compartment with a smaller hatch in the bow. For this reason, larger bulky equipment, like your tent, sleeping bag and personal equipment usually go in the stern hatch while the food goes in the bow hatch. Some kayaks have a small day hatch compartment just behind the cockpit that can be accessed while sitting in the boat on the water. There is also often lots of space inside the cockpit between your feet and the bulkhead, behind and beside the seat and if necessary, between your legs. If you put anything between your feet and the bulkhead, make sure that it will not move and interfere with your use of the foot pedals and that you can get out of the boat easily in case you accidentally capsize. While it is best to pack all the food and equipment inside the kayaks, you may need to carry some cargo on the deck when on longer trips or if you're using smaller boats. This increases your exposure to wind and water and is not recommended, but if you must, tie dry bags securely onto the deck so that they are as streamlined and low-profile as possible.

Be aware of which boats contain fresh produce or bread/meat/cheese so that you can move them to shady spots on warmer days. In the water, the fact that the kayak hull is immersed in water means that food generally keeps quite cool, but depending on temperatures, you might have to keep an eye on certain boats when they are hauled up on land.

HIKING CONSIDERATIONS

Packing for hiking requires you to consider foremost that you'll be carrying it. To minimize back strain, it's best to put the heavier food and equipment as close to your body and as centered as possible. Pack the lighter, bulkier or more easily crushable items at the top. It's also more likely that your pack will be fully unpacked each day, so packing food in chronological order of use is less important, although you'll want to label things very well, and pack all the ingredients required for each meal together. Your priority each morning when packing up is to make sure that your lunch and snacks for that day are easily accessible.

In many cases, if you've waterproofed your food by wrapping things in plastic as we've suggested, these food bags can go directly into the pack. Squeeze as much air as possible out of the plastic because this reduces both the space it will take up as well as chances of spoilage. Keeping each package small will also make it easier to fit all items into your pack. Depending on the size of group and length of trip, it can also make sense to organize food into breakfast, lunch and dinner bags, although this can take up more space.

Spread the food out by meal or by day between each hiker (keeping body size and fitness level in mind) so the loads get progressively and proportionally lighter for everyone. Because a hiking menu should be light and compact, there should be a lot less fresh food and staples to carry, so you might decide that these things are best carried by one person. Each person will also have to take a share of the group equipment and fuel.

BASIC RECIPES

CHAPTER 5

At last – some things to cook for yourself! We'll start with a quick look at how a typical evening might go when you pull into camp and then follow it with a wide range of some of our best recipes for you to enjoy.

For all of our recipes, we have provided the number of portions, alternatives and shortcuts where relevant, approximate preparation time and effort level (I being the easiest; IV being the hardest, loosely based on how whitewater is graded).

THE "TYPICAL" EVENING

Well, you made it! You've arrived at camp with a hearty appetite and are ready to settle in. You know how to start a fire and use your stove. You've got pots, pans and plates. Your food has been water-proofed and organized and is packed away in your boat or back-pack... but the best part is you know it's going to be delicious. So what exactly do you do now? Here's a high-level look at how a typical evening might go:

- arrive at camp

- decide on kitchen, tent, bathroom and gray water areas

- set up tarp in kitchen area if necessary, (while kitchen area is being set up, others can be setting up tents, pumping/filtering water, hauling boats up, collecting firewood)

- set up "table" in kitchen (for example, an overturned canoe or flat rock)

- check menu and locate food for dinner

- get pots and stoves out

- get water from lake or river

- start fire or light stove

- get water on to boil

- make soup and/or start appetizers

- pour some wine or other drinks

- start other dinner preparations (for example, chopping vegetables); some people might prefer to take charge of a certain dish or recipe and follow it through to completion, while other helpers prefer just a simple task like chopping carrots. It does help if one person is keeping an eye on the overall preparation of all the dishes so nothing is missed.

- when all the raw preparation for each dish is complete, establish a "dinner time" and work out the timing for cooking so everything is ready at about the same time

- while cooking is going on, set table and prepare dessert so that it can cook or bake while you're eating dinner (or make the decision to prepare it after dinner)

- as soon as the dinner comes off the fire or stove, use the fire or stove efficiently by putting a pot of water on so that it is ready for dishes and/or for hot drinks after dinner

- serve dinner

- make a toast and dig in!

- if dessert is cooking or baking, check it periodically throughout dinner

- wash dinner dishes (especially if you'll need to use the same ones for dessert)

- if dessert is not cooking or baking, prepare it

- prepare and serve after-dinner drinks (coffee, tea) and dessert

- clean up campsite, pack up food, animal-proof the campsite for the evening

- kick back and enjoy the rest of the evening

- head off to bed, and dream of tomorrow's adventures (and upcoming meals)

BREAKFAST

BREAKFAST on the trail falls into two basic categories: relaxed and slow starts or eat-on-the-go calorie grabs. Regardless of which one you end up doing, remember that breakfast really is the most important meal of the day! When you are spending time in the great outdoors, good fuel in the morning will get your motor running.

FRUIT COMPOTE

This can be a filling breakfast on its own. You can adjust the fruit, the crust and the amount of sweetness to create very different tastes.

Serves 6
30 minutes
Effort Level: II

INGREDIENTS:
- 4 cups (1 L) dried fruit (apricots, pears, apples, prunes, cranberries)
- 4 cups (1 L) water
- 1/2 cup (125 ml) dried applesauce (optional)
- 2 tbsp (30 ml) honey, syrup or sugar (optional)
- 4 cups (1 L) biscuit mix
- 1/2 cup (125 ml) water
- 1/2 cup (125 ml) pecans
- 1 orange, zested and sliced
- 1/4 cup (60 ml) brown sugar
- 1 tbsp (15 ml) butter
- 1 tsp (5 ml) cinnamon

METHOD
To make the compote:
1. Heat the briquettes for the Dutch oven or get your oven ready to bake at 350°F (175°C).
2. Mix the dried fruit and dried applesauce in the Dutch oven and add water until it is just below the top of the fruit. (You may need more or less water, depending on the type of fruit). Most dried fruit will be sweet enough, but add the honey, syrup or sugar to make it sweeter if you like, particularly with tart fruit. The dried applesauce will thicken the compote. For thinner compote, omit the applesauce. You can also thicken the compote with 1/2 cup (125 ml) of flour sprinkled over the fruit just before you make the crust.
3. Bring the fruit mix to a boil. The longer you simmer it the softer the fruit will be, and this is really a matter of preference.

To make the crust:
A plain tea biscuit crust is very nice and will soak up the delicious juice of the compote, but if it's worth doing, it's worth overdoing - so you can make an already impressive dish fancier by dressing up the crust with some extra flavor.
1. Grate the peel of the orange and slice the orange into small pieces.
2. Combine the peel, orange slices and pecans with the dry tea biscuit mix.
3. Add water to the mix until the dough is moist but not sticky.
4. Roll the dough out to the size of the Dutch oven.
5. Spread butter and sprinkle cinnamon and brown sugar on the top of the crust.
6. Place the dough on top of the fruit and bake for 20 to 30 minutes.

DRESS IT UP!
The crust can be rolled and sliced like cinnamon buns and then placed like a mosaic on top of the fruit. Hazelnuts or almonds can be added to the fruit. Instead of sugar and cinnamon on the crust, you can try a bit of honey, orange juice and butter. As always, if there are fresh berries to add to the compote, throw some in!

Tips!
With a thick sauce this can be a very filling dish. With a thinner sauce this mixes well with granola.

COWBOY COFFEE

For many, neither breakfast - nor the day itself - begins until a cup of coffee or tea has been had. Although instant coffee and boiling water is a simple solution, it doesn't come close to delivering the satisfaction derived from freshly brewed java.

Serves 6
5 minutes
Effort level: IV
  In the morning
Effort level: I
  In the evening

METHOD There are a number of ways to make a good pot of coffee on a trip. You can pour boiling water into an unbreakable French-press (Bodum), or through a coffee filter into a pot or cup, but these don't appeal to me because they are the same old things you would do at home. I concede that there is some appeal to the old-school percolator with the glass knob on top. You can see the water turn from pale tea-colored liquid to rich brown elixir. There is nothing like waking to the sound of a crackling fire and that percolating noise, which is not unlike a bullfrog gargling.

However, of all these methods I prefer to use a tall coffee pot without the percolating apparatus, in which I'll boil water. Once boiled, I add fresh ground coffee (the same grind as you'd use for a percolator) using about a heaping tablespoon per cup and an extra one for the pot. (Not even mathematicians can successfully dispute this irrational and inconsistent ratio.) But already this sounds too much like a recipe, and cowboy coffee is an art. What I usually do (knowing the size of my pot and having done it many times) is instead of measuring anything, I'll carefully pour three cupped handfuls into the pot of freshly boiled water. After several minutes, I'll swing the pot in big circles to settle the grounds at the bottom of the pot using centrifugal force. The first quick splash from the pot goes on the ground in respectful sacrifice to the coffee gods (and to avoid a mouthful of floating grounds). The few remaining grounds lend back-country authenticity. The inconsistency of this system gives the coffee connoisseurs in the group an opportunity to ruminate and pontificate at length about the quality of each particular brew.

-Mark Scriver

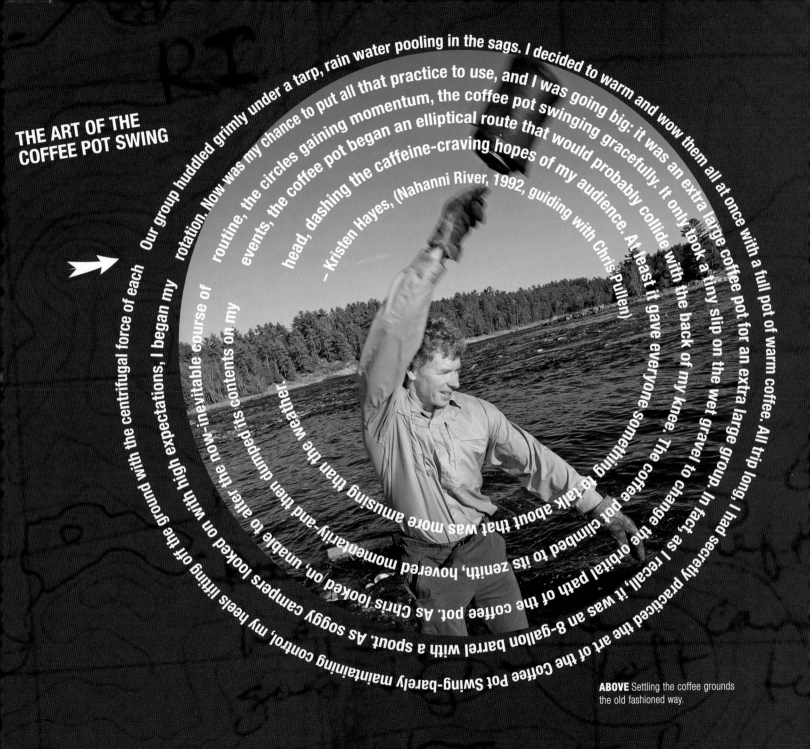

THE ART OF THE COFFEE POT SWING

Our group huddled grimly under a tarp, rain water pooling in the sags. I decided to warm and wow them all at once with a full pot of warm coffee. All trip long, I had secretly practiced the art of the Coffee Pot Swing—barely maintaining control, my heels lifting off the ground with the centrifugal force of each rotation. Now was my chance to put all that practice to use, and I was going big: it was an extra large coffee pot for an extra large group. In fact, as I recall, it was an 8-gallon barrel with a spout. As Chris looked on, unable to alter the now-inevitable course of events, the coffee pot began an elliptical route that would probably collide with the back of my knee. The coffee pot climbed to its zenith, hovered momentarily—and then dumped its contents on my head, dashing the caffeine-craving hopes of my audience. At least it gave everyone something to talk about. As soggy campers looked on, the circles gaining momentum, the coffee pot swinging gracefully. It only took a tiny slip on the wet gravel to change the orbital path of the coffee pot, the coffee pot was more amusing than the weather.

I began my routine,

— Kristen Hayes, (Nahanni River, 1992, guiding with Chris Pullen)

ABOVE Settling the coffee grounds the old fashioned way.

OATMEAL

Serves 6
10 minutes
Effort Level: I

DRESS IT UP!

Fresh fruit and/or chopped nuts are a tasty addition and a good way to cover your food groups for breakfast. Cinnamon, nutmeg and vanilla can be used to make it taste more gourmet. Try a couple of tablespoons of molasses and a tablespoon of peanut butter.

Tips!

You'll often have people trickle in for breakfast. Cold and thickened oatmeal isn't very appealing, but leaving it on the heat will burn the bottom. Put a lid on the oatmeal pot and place it in a larger pot of almost boiling water. A stone in the water pot will keep the water out of the oatmeal pot and the hot water will keep the oatmeal warm without burning the bottom.

VARIATIONS!

Cream of wheat, Red River Cereal, cornmeal and multigrain cereals are similar to oatmeal, but have different tastes and textures and cooking times. Use about 1/4 cup (60 ml) of these cereals per person per one cup of boiling water. For best results, add the grains slowly to vigorously boiling water and cook for 10 to 15 minutes.

This is a pretty easy one, and the directions are on the oatmeal package if you don't trust us. Oatmeal is basically whole grain oats flattened after the hulls have been removed. Quick cooking oats are just cut and flattened more. Oats are a good source of fiber and carbohydrates, and when combined with milk they form a more complete protein so we recommend that you either mix up some powdered milk to serve with it or simply stir milk or milk powder into the oats as they are cooking. As with all grains, a pinch of salt will bring out the flavor of the grain.

Oatmeal tastes fine on its own but it is also a good vehicle for adding other ingredients to add more flavor and nutrition.

METHOD

1. Bring the water to a boil in a medium pot. Add salt and stir in the rolled oats. If you're adding dried fruit now is a good time so it will rehydrate.
2. Cook until the grains have swollen to their full capacity or to suit your taste; between a couple of minutes for quick-cooking oats and around 10 minutes for well-cooked large-flake oats. Stir occasionally to keep the oats from sticking to the bottom of the pot.
3. If you're adding milk powder you can add it slowly to the pot in the last minute of cooking. Stir constantly as you add it to avoid clumps from forming or mix the milk powder in 1/2 cup (125 ml) of cold water and add it to the pot. Some like oatmeal stiff and some like it runny, so adjust the amount of water to suit your taste. Serve with brown sugar or maple syrup and milk.

INGREDIENTS:
- 6 cups (1 1/2 L) water
- 3 cups (750 ml) rolled oats
- 1/2 cup (125 ml) raisins and/or dried fruit
- pinch salt
- 1/4 cup (60 ml) milk powder, maple syrup or brown sugar, to taste

PEACHES AND CREAM
OF WHEAT

Serves 6

15 minutes

Effort Level: I

INGREDIENTS:
- 2 cups (500 ml) cream of wheat
- 6 cups (1 1/2 L) water
- 1/4 cup (60 ml) milk powder
- 1/2 cup (125 ml) dehydrated peaches, chopped

This recipe imitates the packaged peaches and cream oatmeal you can buy. The store-bought stuff contains lots of artificial flavors and chemicals. This is the natural alternative and really easy to make.

METHOD
1. Boil the water and add the cream of wheat. Stir frequently to avoid lumps.
2. Cook until it reaches the thickness you like and remove from heat.
3. Add peaches and milk powder, then serve.

DRESS IT UP!
Drizzle each serving with maple syrup.

BLACK FEATHER
MUESLI

Serves 6

20 minutes

Effort Level: II

INGREDIENTS:
- 3 cups (750 ml) muesli mix
- 1/2 cup (125 ml) freeze-dried applesauce
- 20 oz (590 ml) canned fruit cocktail with juice
- 6 oz (185 ml) 1% evaporated milk
- 1 cup (250 ml) milk, made from powder

Original Swiss-style muesli is an uncooked breakfast made by soaking rolled oats in yogurt, apples and water overnight, then adding nuts, dried fruit and spices. Black Feather's variation starts with a basic muesli mix that can be found at any bulk food store, but we add other ingredients to make a tasty, nutritious breakfast cereal. It is best to start preparations the night before, but it's also okay to mix it all up in the morning.

METHOD In a stainless steel bowl, mix all ingredients together, except extra milk. Cover, and let stand overnight (or for 20 minutes). Add extra milk to bring mixture to the consistency of oatmeal (not too thick, not too runny).

DRESS IT UP!
Add any fresh fruit that is available or yogurt if you are early in the trip.

WHOLE WHEAT PANCAKES

Serves 6

15-20 minutes – depending on how many you cook!

Effort Level: I

INGREDIENTS:
- 3 cups (750 ml) whole wheat flour
- 2 tsp (10 ml) baking powder
- 3/4 tsp (4 ml) cinnamon
- 6 tsp (30 ml) vegetable oil
- 3 tbsp (45 ml) egg powder
- 3 cups (750 ml) milk, made from powder

Pancakes are always a great way to start the day. They're fun to make, fun to flip and fun to eat. With a larger group, it's great to have a griddle so that you can make a few at a time and keep the production line going! I like to cook a few extra at breakfast time and save them for lunch because leftover pancakes topped with peanut butter and jam are a delectable treat!

- Chris Harris

METHOD

1. Before the trip, combine flour, baking powder, cinnamon, and egg powder and store in plastic bag. On your trip, in large bowl, combine dry ingredients with oil.
2. Add milk and stir until you have a soupy mix. You can change the consistency by adjusting the amount of milk that you add.
3. Heat the griddle with some oil, hot enough to make water droplets dance.
4. Spoon circles of pancake mix onto the griddle. Fry on one side until bubbles form on the surface and the edges dry out slightly.
5. Flip the pancakes and cook them for about half the time needed for the first side.

DRESS IT UP!

If you have fresh eggs available, use three instead of the egg powder - just beat them first. If you want fluffier pancakes, separate the eggs. Add the yolks when you add the milk. Then whisk the whites until they are foamy and gently fold them into the batter just before frying.

If you are in a place where you can pick fresh berries, by all means add them to the mix. You can also bring dehydrated blueberries.

Top with real maple syrup or squeeze a bit of fresh lemon and then sprinkle them with icing sugar.

Tips!

Make sure your griddle is pre-heated and well-oiled. Fire (or stove flame) should be at a medium heat to prevent burning. Resist the temptation to squish the pancakes down by pressing on them with your spatula - give them the chance to rise and get fluffy!

FRENCH TOAST

Serves 6
20 minutes
Effort Level: II

INGREDIENTS:
- 1 cup (250 ml) egg powder
- 1 1/2 cups (375 ml) water
- 2 tsp (10 ml) cinnamon
- 1 loaf bread, sliced
- maple syrup, to taste

This is a tasty standard that works well with egg powder.

METHOD

1. Mix the egg powder, water and cinnamon. The mixture should be just slightly thicker than milk so that the batter sticks to the bread but doesn't leave a thick coating.
2. Heat a greased griddle or frying pan to a medium heat.
3. Dunk the bread in the egg mixture and fry until golden brown. Serve with maple syrup.

Tips!

Use soft bread that will soak up the egg so that the center will have a custard-like consistency. Add a little vanilla to the mix for a different flavor.

GREAT GRANOLA

Serves 12
40 minutes - make prior to trip
Effort Level: II

INGREDIENTS:
- 6 cups (1 1/2 L) whole rolled oats
- 1 cup (250 ml) sunflower seeds
- 1 cup (250 ml) wheat germ
- 1/2 cup (125 ml) wheat bran
- 3/4 cup (175 ml) maple syrup
- 3/4 cup (175 ml) vegetable or extra virgin olive oil
- 1/2 tsp (2 ml) salt
- 1 tbsp (15 ml) vanilla
- 1 cup (250 ml) almonds, chopped
- 1 cup (250 ml) dried cranberries
- 1 cup (250 ml) dried blueberries

Outdoor enthusiasts are often called "granolas" - so this is a recipe for us! Make it before the trip and it will be ready to serve with milk or yogurt.

- Theresa Bernier

METHOD

1. In a large bowl, mix all the dry ingredients except for the cranberries, blueberries, and chopped almonds.
2. In another bowl, mix the wet ingredients and stir well.
3. Combine the wet and dry ingredients and spread the mixture evenly over four baking sheets.
4. Bake at 350° F (175°C) for 8 minutes.
5. Remove each tray from the oven and stir the granola so it doesn't stick together in clumps and return it to the oven for 8 more minutes.
6. Add the chopped almonds and bake for another 10 minutes, or until the oats and almonds are lightly toasted. Remove from oven and allow to cool completely.
7. Add the cranberries and blueberries. Store the granola in airtight container or baggies.

DRESS IT UP!

Serve Great Granola with a dollop of low-fat plain yogurt, skim milk and sliced fresh strawberries!

Tips!

Stir the mixture well during cooking to make sure that everything gets evenly toasted.

CRANBERRY ALMOND MUFFINS

DRESS IT UP!

Drizzle honey over the wedges or serve with butterscotch or lemon sauce.

Tips!

Watch the heat in the last five minutes or so of baking. A minute or two can make the difference between perfection and black bottoms. If you do over-bake the muffins, simply slice the blackened bits off and serve.

VARIATIONS!

The spices, fruit and nuts are all optional of course. This is a very flexible recipe and you can add whatever fruit, nuts and spices you like. Two over-ripe bananas are a great replacement for the cranberries and nuts - just mash them up first.

Here is a versatile recipe for a surprisingly easy breakfast. There are store-bought mixes that are quite acceptable or you can mix your own muffin ingredients at home and just add the water and oil at the campsite.

Preparation and cook time is surprisingly short. As with most breakfast baking, producing fresh muffins by stumbling out of your tent 25 minutes ahead of everyone else can elevate you to hero status, and might even get you out of doing dishes for a few days. This recipe will make the equivalent of 12 medium-sized muffins, but muffin pans aren't that efficient so we cook them in a round pan in an Outback Oven or Dutch oven.

METHOD

1. Heat the briquettes for the Dutch oven or get your oven ready to bake at 350°F (175°C).
2. Rehydrate the cranberries in hot water for 5 minutes while you grease the Dutch oven or baking pan.
3. Mix the dry ingredients and then add the liquid. Stir only until the mixture is wet.
4. Pour the batter into the greased Dutch oven or baking pan and bake for about 20 minutes.

It's done when a clean twig stuck into the batter comes out without batter sticking to it, or when the top rebounds to a light touch. It *is* easier to slice into six wedges if you wait a few minutes until it cools, but who has time for that?

Serves 6
25 minutes
Effort Level: II

INGREDIENTS:
- 2 cups (500 ml) whole wheat flour
- 1/2 tsp (2 ml) salt
- 4 tsp (20 ml) baking powder
- 3/4 cup (175 ml) brown sugar
- 1/2 cup (125 ml) dried cranberries
- 1/4 cup (60 ml) slivered almonds
- 1/2 cup (125 ml) canola oil
- 1/4 cup (60 ml) milk powder
- 1/2 cup (125 ml) egg powder
- 1 cup (250 ml) water
- 2 tsp (10 ml) vanilla

BASIC BISCUITS

There is nothing like a fresh biscuit with butter to start the day. This is one of those recipes that should serve as a starting point for your creativity. Use the ingredients you have on hand to create variations of this recipe.

You can combine the dry ingredients before the trip. Remember to label the bag well and include a note to remind you what else needs to be added and the instructions.

Serves 6

45 minutes

Effort Level: III

INGREDIENTS:
- 2 1/2 cups (625 ml) all purpose flour
- 1 tbsp (15 ml) baking powder
- 1/2 tsp (2 ml) salt
- 1 tbsp (15 ml) sugar
- 1/2 cup (125 ml) butter or margarine
- 1/4 cup (60 ml) milk powder
- 3/4 cup (175 ml) water
- 1/2 cup (125 ml) egg powder

METHOD

1. Heat the briquettes for the Dutch oven or get your oven ready to bake at 350°F (175°C).
2. In a large bowl, mix together the flour, baking powder, salt and sugar.
3. Cut the butter into the dry ingredients until the mixture resembles coarse crumbs.
4. Add milk powder and egg powder, and then stir in water until just combined. (The texture should be sticky, moist and lumpy.) Add more water if necessary.
5. Place mixture on a lightly floured surface and knead dough gently until it comes together and becomes smooth.
6. Roll out dough to 1/2 inch (1 1/4 cm) thickness. At this point you can divide them into separate biscuits using a knife or the rim of a cup, or place the dough as one piece in a greased Dutch oven or baking pan.
7. Bake for about 10 minutes or until the top is golden brown and a clean twig inserted in the center comes out clean. Serve warm with butter.

DRESS IT UP!

Add dried cranberries and lemon zest to the dry ingredients and sprinkle white sugar over the biscuits before you bake them. You can also add fresh or dried blueberries.

BUTTERSCOTCH OR LEMON SAUCE

This sauce is an easy way to dress up muffins on a cold day, or it can be used in place of syrup for pancakes, but it is better known as a sauce for steamed puddings or spice cakes. There are many ways to make a butterscotch sauce but I learned this recipe from my mother. Christmas dinner would always conclude with steamed plum pudding and this sauce.

Serves 6
10 minutes
Effort Level: I

INGREDIENTS (BUTTERSCOTCH):
- 1 1/2 cups (375 ml) brown sugar
- 1 1/2 cups (375 ml) water, boiled
- 2 tbsp (30 ml) corn starch
- 1/4 cup (60 ml) cold water
- 2 tbsp (30 ml) butter
- 1 tsp (5 ml) vanilla
- splash almond liquor

METHOD

1. Heat the brown sugar in a pan, stirring constantly. It will start to melt.
2. Add the boiling water and stir until the sugar is dissolved.
3. Add the corn starch to the cold water and stir until it is completely dissolved and then add to the pan. Add the butter and vanilla and stir for about 3 or 4 minutes until the sauce thickens and the starchy taste disappears. Keep the sauce just below the boiling point as it thickens.

Variation: Lemon Sauce
My mother also makes a sweet lemon sauce that serves the same general purpose: to make desserts taste even better.

METHOD

1. Mix together the sugar and the corn starch.
2. Add the boiling water. Stir and cook until the mixture starts to bubble.
3. Remove from heat and add the butter, then stir in the zest and juice from half a lemon.

INGREDIENTS (LEMON SAUCE):
- 1/4 cup (60 ml) white sugar
- 1 tbsp (15 ml) corn starch
- 1 cup (250 ml) water, boiled
- 2 tbsp (30 ml) butter
- 1/2 lemon, juice and zest

PUDDING ON THE DUMOINE

On a late fall trip down the Dumoine River in Quebec, we had cold, wet and miserable weather. Without a lot of daylight, we were cooking most of our meals in the dark. I had brought a home-baked plum pudding wrapped in wax paper and tinfoil - the wax paper to keep the pudding from acquiring the metallic taste of the foil. I put some stones in a pot of boiling water to keep the pudding out of the water. It warmed and steamed nicely in 15 minutes. We made the butterscotch sauce, laced it with amaretto and served it with the pudding. Sauce usually means a quarter cup drizzled over whatever you've baked, but our pudding was swimming in a bowl full of steaming sauce. Just as we sat down to enjoy our dessert by candlelight under the tarp the rain turned to fat snowflakes.

– Mark Scriver

CINNAMON BUNS

You will be everyone's favorite person if you pull off freshly baked cinnamon buns on a cold morning. This recipe requires baking but the cook time is not too long and they taste so good that it's worth the effort. Serve up a first course like granola with dried fruit while the buns are baking. By the time someone says "that was good, but I'm still hungry", you'll be ready to present the group with a plate of warm cinnamon buns! If you time the pouring of the coffee just right, they might let you carry the light packs for the day.

This recipe has a short-cut option to use biscuit mix instead of making the dough from scratch, depending on your preference. (See below.)

METHOD Heat the briquettes for the Dutch oven or get your oven ready to bake at 350°F (175°C).

To make the dough:
1. In a large bowl, mix together the flour, baking powder, salt and sugar.
2. Use a fork or two knives to cut the butter into the dry ingredients until the mixture resembles coarse crumbs.
3. Add milk powder, water and egg powder and stir until just combined. The texture should be pliable but fairly firm, not sticky. Add a little more water or flour if necessary.
4. Place mixture on a lightly floured surface (like a cutting board or the clean bottom of a canoe) and knead the dough gently until it comes together and becomes smooth.

To assemble the cinnamon buns:
1. Use a smooth-sided water bottle to roll out the dough into a rectangle that is about 1/2 inch (a little over 1 cm) thick.
2. Spread (or if the butter is hard, slice thinly and scatter) butter across the dough, leaving about 1 inch (2 1/2 cm) bare at one end. (You need this bare end to seal the end of the cinnamon bun roll in Step 4.)

Short Cut!

Instead of making the dough from scratch as described above, you can use a store-bought biscuit mix that requires you to just add water. Use approximately 4 cups (1 L) of the dry mix and adjust the amount of water or mix to make the dough pliable but fairly firm (not sticky).

Serves 6
45 minutes
Effort Level: III

INGREDIENTS:
Dough
- 4 1/4 cups (1060 ml) all purpose flour
- 2 tbsp (30 ml) baking powder
- 1 tsp (5 ml) salt
- 1/4 cup (60 ml) sugar
- 1/2 cup (125 ml) butter or margarine
- 1/2 cup (125 ml) milk powder
- 1 1/2 cups (375 ml) water

Filling
- 2 tbsp (30 ml) butter or margarine
- 1/2 cup (125 ml) brown sugar
- 2 tsp (5 ml) cinnamon
- 3/4 cup (60 ml) nuts (optional)
- 3/4 cup (60 ml) raisins (optional)

DRESS IT UP!

Gently warm and drizzle cream cheese over the cinnamon buns to really blow your friends away!

VARIATIONS!

This is a pretty quick and very popular breakfast so you may want to repeat it with variations, like the date filling listed here. Try making fillings using different fresh or dried fruits, nuts and sweeteners. More moisture in the filling will increase the cooking time by up to 5 minutes. You can even layer the rolls over fruit compote. Another option is to make the rolls savory with cheese and herbs as a filling – then bake them on top of vegetables or stew or Turkey Pot Pie.

3. Sprinkle remaining ingredients evenly across the dough, once again leaving 1 inch (2 1/2 cm) bare at one end.
4. Roll the dough into a long sausage toward the bare end, and then gently pinch the end into the side of the roll to seal it.
5. With a sharp knife, cut the dough roll into slices that are about 1 inch (2 1/2 cm) thick. Lay the slices (they can be touching or not) in a greased baking pan or Dutch oven.
6. Bake for 15 to 20 minutes, or until the tops are golden brown and a clean twig inserted in the center comes out clean. Serve warm!

Variation: Date Filling
METHOD
1. Over low heat, soften the pitted dates with the orange juice, stirring to prevent burning.
2. Add the grated peel and molasses (optional).
3. Use as the filling in the cinnamon bun recipe, replacing the brown sugar, nuts and raisins.

INGREDIENTS:
Date Filling
- 1 1/2 cup (375 ml) pitted dates
- 2 tbsp (30 ml) orange juice
- 1 tbsp (15 ml) molasses (optional)
- 1 tbsp (15 ml) grated orange peel (optional)

SPICY EGG BURRITOS

This is a great breakfast - tasty, a good source of protein, and the spices disguise the fact that it uses dried eggs!

Serves 6

15 minutes

Effort Level: II

INGREDIENTS:
- 2 cups (500 ml) egg powder
- 2 cups (500 ml) milk, made from powder
- 3 tbsp (45 ml) olive oil
- 1 green or red pepper, diced, or 1 cup (250 ml) dried peppers
- 1 tsp (5 ml) dried basil
- 9 oz (250 g) cheddar cheese, grated
- 1 cup (250 ml) salsa
- 12 flour tortillas

METHOD

1. Combine the egg powder, milk, basil and if you are using rehydrated red and green pepper, throw those in as well.
2. Heat the oil in a wok or skillet. If you're using fresh peppers, sauté them and then add the egg mixture. You can stir occasionally, or let it cook slowly and flip it all at once.
3. While the eggs are cooking, warm the tortillas on a dry, ungreased griddle or frying pan over medium heat. Less than a minute per side is required to soften and warm them, and prevent them from cracking when you try to fold them.
4. Spoon a small amount of egg mixture onto each tortilla and top with some grated cheese and a spoonful of salsa, then fold them up like envelopes.
5. Place the folded tortillas on the ungreased griddle over medium heat, and heat both sides until tortillas are golden and cheese melted.

DRESS IT UP!

In Mexico, this would be accompanied by warmed refried beans and extra salsa on the side. A few slices of honeydew melon and cantaloupe add freshness and color.

Tips!

By using a griddle, you can cook lots of burritos at the same time and nobody has to wait.

If you want something a little spicier, add a few pinches of chili powder to the egg mixture, or provide some hot sauce on the side.

HOME FRIES

This is a stick-to-your-ribs favorite on chilly days.

DRESS IT UP!

Chop up and add a can of cooked ham while warming or a little cheese can be shredded over top just before the fries come off the stove or fire.

Tips!

If time is a factor, put a splash of water in before adding the potatoes, then cover and reduce the heat. The potatoes will heat up more quickly without getting too mashed.

METHOD

1. Boil the potatoes and sweet potato the night before until they are just cooked. Drain and leave them in the pot overnight. (If you put the lid on tight and pack them carefully, the pot will sit safely in the top of a closed food barrel or at the top of a food pack.)
2. Fry the onion and green pepper in the oil.
3. Add the spices and the rest of ingredients and stir until they've warmed up and started going a little brown. Serve with hot pepper sauce or chili sauce.

Serves 6
20 minutes
Effort Level: I

INGREDIENTS:
- 1/2 onion, diced
- 1 green or red pepper, diced, or 1 cup (250 ml) dried peppers
- 2 tbsp (30 ml) vegetable oil
- 4 potatoes, cubed
- 1 sweet potato, cubed
- 2 cloves garlic
- 1 tsp (5 ml) black pepper
- 1 tsp (5 ml) parsley

LUNCH

LUNCHES on trips are usually a casual buffet of spreads, meats, cheeses, condiments and vegetables. This section will offer a few things to make lunches reliably delicious.

There are also many different types of prepared bean and vegetable spreads available at your grocery store or specialty food shop, including hummus (made from chick peas), baba ghanoush (grilled eggplant), roasted red pepper, bean or carrot spread, and olive tapenade. Many of these go well on lunch sandwiches, crackers or served as dip for raw vegetables for appetizers. Most of these dips will keep for several days, depending on the type of vegetable and the temperatures they are exposed to. Some of these spreads are available dehydrated, or you can

always make your own spreads at home and dehydrate them before the trip. If you make your own spreads and dehydrate them, it's often best to omit the oil and add it on the trip.

Peanut butter and jam or honey is another popular lunch because it delivers just what an active body wants (protein and carbohydrates) and it tastes great. As an alternative to peanut butter, try almond butter, hazelnut butter or cashew butter. On the sweet side, there are some nut-based spreads like halva (made from sesame paste) and Nutella (hazelnut and chocolate).

Don't forget, some people love vegemite and marmite... and these are excellent sources of B vitamins.

HUMMUS

METHOD

1. Add water until you have the desired consistency. It can take a few minutes for the water to be fully absorbed, so you may have to add a bit more.
2. Stir in fresh minced garlic, lemon juice and olive oil.

DRESS IT UP!

Sprinkle a few herbs and paprika on top, and drizzle a swirl of olive oil.

VARIATIONS!

Feel free to make your own hummus at home, leaving out the olive oil, lemon juice and garlic, then dehydrate it before the trip. When you reconstitute the hummus with water, you can add these missing ingredients.

Serves 6
2 minutes
Effort Level: I

INGREDIENTS:
- 1 1/2 cups (375 ml) dehydrated hummus
- 1 cup (250 ml) water
- lemon juice to taste (optional)
- olive oil to taste (optional)
- 1 clove garlic, minced (optional)

CURRY CHEDDAR SPREAD

Serves 6

15 minutes

Effort Level: I

INGREDIENTS:
- 3 cups (750 ml) cheddar cheese, shredded
- 4 tbsp (60 ml) mayonnaise or substitute
- 1 tbsp (15 ml) curry powder

This is one of those things I would never eat at home because I would be put off by the high fat content, but it is a delicious treat and perfectly acceptable to eat after a long day of outdoor activity! This simple spread is fantastic on crackers, stuffed in pita or on regular bread, and can be used to make sandwiches extra-delicious.

- Joanna Baker

METHOD
1. Mix all the ingredients and serve!

Tips!
Unrefrigerated real mayonnaise will go bad pretty quickly, but Miracle Whip "Salad Dressing" tastes almost the same and will last months.

If you prefer real mayonnaise, you can get small take-out size packages that don't need to be refrigerated.

DRESS IT UP!
Use extra old white cheddar and it will take this dip up to a whole new level.

TUNA OR SALMON SALAD

Tips!

You can use dehydrated canned salmon or tuna; simply start soaking the fish before lunch so that it is rehydrated by the time you are ready to eat.

See the tip about mayonnaise in the recipe for Curry Cheddar Spread.

This lunch spread goes well on any kind of bread.

METHOD
1. Mix ingredients in a bowl and serve!

Variation: Salmon salad

METHOD
1. Try this slight variation using canned salmon instead of canned tuna.

Serves 6
2 minutes
Effort Level: I

INGREDIENTS:
- 13 oz (360 g) 3 cans of tuna
- 1/2 cup (125 ml) mayonnaise or substitute
- 1/2 cup (125 ml) celery, diced
- 1/2 tsp (2 ml) dried parsley
- 1/2 tsp (2 ml) dried oregano
- 1 tbsp (15 ml) lemon juice

Salmon Variation
- 13 oz (360 g) 3 cans of salmon
- 1/2 cup (125 ml) mayonnaise or substitute
- 1/2 cup (125 ml) red onion, finely diced
- 1/4 cup (60 ml) pickles, finely diced
- 1/2 tsp (2 ml) dried parsley
- 1 tsp (5 ml) lemon juice

CHICKEN AND MANDARIN PASTA SALAD

Pasta, rice or legume salads are a filling alternative to sandwiches.

METHOD

1. Cook and rinse the macaroni, then drizzle with a bit of oil.
2. Chop the chicken and then combine it with the macaroni, red pepper, carrots and oranges.
3. In a separate container, mix the olive oil, balsamic vinegar, mandarin juice, garlic and dry mustard and then add it to the salad.

Tips!

If you're serving this for lunch you can cook the macaroni in the morning or the night before, then let it cool and store it in a clean bag so that it's ready for lunch. Add a bit of oil after cooking and rinsing to avoid it turning to one big clump.

VARIATIONS!

Get creative by using different spicing combinations, like adding curry and a bit of basil and tossing in some almonds or other nuts.

Serves 6
5 minutes (with pre-cooked macaroni)
Effort Level: II

INGREDIENTS:
- 28 oz (800 g) canned chicken
- 16 oz (450 g) canned mandarin oranges
- 3 cups (750 ml) dry macaroni
- 1/2 cup (125 ml) red pepper, sliced
- 1/2 cup (125 ml) carrots, sliced
- 1/4 cup (60 ml) olive oil
- 1 tbsp (15 ml) balsamic vinegar
- 1/4 cup (60 ml) juice from mandarin oranges
- 1 tsp (5 ml) garlic, minced
- 1/2 tsp (2 ml) dry mustard

MEDITERRANEAN POTATO SALAD

Serves 6
30 minutes
Effort Level: III

INGREDIENTS:
- 3 medium white potatoes
- 1/2 cup (125 ml) olive oil
- 1 tsp (5 ml) dried basil
- 4 tbsp (60 ml) balsamic vinegar
- 1 clove garlic, minced
- 1 onion, chopped
- 1/2 cup (125 ml) sundried tomatoes in oil, chopped
- 1/2 cup (125 ml) black olives, chopped
- 1/4 cup (60 ml) capers
- 1/4 cup (60 ml) pine nuts
- salt and pepper to taste

I first ate this potato salad sitting on a pier looking out onto the Saguenay River with two really good friends. We were heading out on a sea kayaking trip and one was pregnant with her first baby. It was a beautiful summer day and we were giddy with the thought of slipping our boats into the water and beginning our adventure. You can make this potato salad the night before and have it for lunch or do what we did and pre-pack it for the first day's picnic.

- Joanna Baker

METHOD

1. Scrub the potatoes and cube them into bite-sized pieces.
2. Boil the potatoes until just cooked. Drain.
3. Mix together the olive oil, dried basil, vinegar and garlic to create the dressing.
4. Mix the onion, sundried tomatoes, olives, capers and pine nuts and toss with the dressing.
5. Add salt and pepper to taste.

DRESS IT UP!
Grate some fresh parmesan cheese on top of the salad or add crumbled feta.

SNACKS

SNACKS are mandatory for keeping blood sugar (and spirits) steady on active days in the outdoors. Here are a few of our favorites that you can share with your group.

FRUIT LEATHER

Fruit leather is one of the easiest things to make in a food dehydrator. The recipe is very flexible and forgiving - more than exact quantities, you are really just looking for the right consistency and sweetness. Apples are high in pectin, which helps the fruit leather hold together and turn out nice and chewy, so applesauce is used as the foundation ingredient.

You can make plain apple leather, or you can add 2-4 cups of other fruit to make different flavors. Because the fruit will be dehydrated, it is not necessary to use fresh fruit; you can use frozen or canned just as easily and with similar results.

- Debbie Higgins and Rebecca Sandiford

METHOD

1. In a large bowl, stir together the apple sauce, honey and lemon juice. Stir it well until everything is blended.
2. If you are adding other fruit, use a blender (hand-held or regular) to puree it into the applesauce. If you like sweeter leather, add a little more honey; if you like lemony leather, add more lemon juice. The puree should be about the same consistency as applesauce or slightly thicker.
3. Ladle the puree or applesauce onto waxed or parchment paper dehydrator trays, spreading it carefully so that it is about a 1/4 inch (1/2 cm) thick. Because dehydrators are all different, do your first batch when you can check it every hour or so. Some will take only 1-2 hours; others will take up to 5 or 6, possibly longer. Similarly, it can make a difference to drying time if you are making several trays at once or just one or two.
4. The leather is done if you can press it with a finger tip without leaving an indentation. If you over-dry the leather, it will be brittle, but still tasty.

INGREDIENTS:
- 2 16-oz jars (950 ml) unsweetened apple sauce
- 1/4 cup (50 ml) liquid honey
- 1 tbsp (15 ml) lemon juice

Tips!

This recipe is easy to double or even triple if you want to make huge batches. If your dehydrator doesn't have enough solid trays to accommodate all the leather you're making, you can trace and cut out circles of waxed or parchment paper and lay them over top of the mesh trays.

VARIATIONS!

Options include drained, canned peaches or pears (drain up to two large cans); thawed-from-frozen blueberries, mangos, strawberries, bananas or other fruit; and combinations of fruits like blueberry/pear and mango/peach.

A tablespoon or two of peanut butter (or other nut butter) added to the pureed fruit adds a nice nutty flavor to the leather as well as a bit of protein.

PEPPERED PECANS

This is a snack to prepare before the trip. These provide much needed calories, protein and salt for active people!

DRESS IT UP!
Serve these with the river-chilled six pack of beer that you have been hiding until the perfect moment!

METHOD

1. Preheat oven to 250°F (120°C).
2. Melt butter in a small skillet and add hot sauce, garlic and salt. Sauté for 1 minute.
3. Toss pecans in the butter mixture and spread the nuts in a single layer on a baking sheet.
4. Bake pecans for about 1 hour or until pecans are crisp, stirring every 10 to 15 minutes.

Serves 6
60 minutes
Effort Level: II

INGREDIENTS:
- 3 tbsp (45 ml) butter
- 3 cloves minced garlic
- 1 tsp (5 ml) hot sauce
- 1/2 tsp (2 ml) salt
- 3 cups (750 ml) pecan halves

SPICED NUTS

This is another great recipe to prepare before a trip. Use pecans, peanuts, cashews, or a mixture of nuts.

METHOD

1. Toast the nuts by spreading them in a single layer on a baking sheet and baking in a 350°F (175°C) oven for 10 to 15 minutes, stirring occasionally. You can also toast the nuts by stirring them over medium heat in an ungreased skillet until they are golden brown and aromatic.
2. Combine sugar, salt, nutmeg, cinnamon, cloves, butter, vanilla and water in a saucepan.
3. Cook over medium-high heat stirring constantly until a small amount dropped into cold water forms a soft ball, about 236°F (113°C) on a candy thermometer.
4. Stir in toasted nuts and remove from heat.
5. Stir until the mixture is no longer glossy. Pour onto a buttered baking sheet and spread thinly. Let cool completely, then break into pieces.

Serves 6
30 minutes
Effort Level: II

INGREDIENTS:
- 2 cups (500 ml) sugar
- 1/2 tsp (2 ml) salt
- 1/4 tsp (1 ml) ground nutmeg
- 1 tsp (5 ml) ground cinnamon
- 1/8 tsp (1/2 ml) ground cloves
- 6 tbsp (90 ml) butter
- 6 tbsp (90 ml) water
- 3 cups (750 ml) nuts

PEANUT BUTTER FUDGE

Fudge is easy to make at home, perfect for transporting on trips and a little goes a long way for satisfying a sweet tooth. Fudge made with peanut butter has the added benefit of providing a little bit of protein.

Serves 6

15 minutes

Effort Level: I

INGREDIENTS:
- 1/2 cup (125 ml) butter
- 2 1/4 cups (550 ml) brown sugar
- 1/2 cup (125 ml) milk
- 3/4 cup (175 ml) peanut butter
- 1 tsp (5 ml) vanilla
- 3 1/2 cups (875 ml) powdered sugar

METHOD
1. Melt butter in a medium saucepan over medium heat.
2. Stir in brown sugar and milk. Bring to a boil and boil for 2 minutes, stirring frequently.
3. Remove from heat. Stir in peanut butter and vanilla.
4. Pour over powdered sugar in a large mixing bowl. Beat until smooth, then pour into an 8-inch square dish.
5. Chill until firm, and then cut into squares and pack.

GRANOLA BARS

Although there are a lot of packaged granola bars out there, I really enjoy making my own for trips. I remember sleeping with these bars inside my sleeping bag and cracking into them on particularly cold nights on a winter camping trip north of Thunder Bay. It was always funny to hear my shelter mates gnawing on bars next to me as we attempted to keep enough calories in us to stay warm.

- Joanna Baker

DRESS IT UP!
Substitute cranberries for raisins and add some chopped candied ginger. You can also make a sweeter version by adding chocolate chips.

METHOD
1. In a large bowl combine wheat germ, rolled oats, coconut, raisins, cashews, almonds and sesame seeds.
2. Heat oil, honey, vanilla and maple syrup in a small pot until the liquid is thin. Remove from heat and pour over the dry ingredients. Stir well.
3. Press into two 8-inch square pans and bake at 300°F (150°C) for 30-40 minutes or until brown in color.
4. Cut the bars into squares while they are still hot but then wait to remove them from the pan until they are just warm. Remove when completely cooled and wrap individual servings.

Serves 6
35 minutes
Effort Level: III

INGREDIENTS:
- 1 cup (250 ml) wheat germ
- 6 cups (750 ml) rolled oats
- 1 cup (250 ml) coconut
- 2 cups (500 ml) raisins
- 1 cup (250 ml) chopped cashews
- 1 cup (250 ml) chopped almonds
- 1 cup (250 ml) sesame seeds
- 1/2 cup (125 ml) canola oil
- 1/2 cup (125 ml) honey
- 1/2 cup (125 ml) maple syrup
- 1 tbsp (15 ml) vanilla

JERKY – BEEF OR TURKEY

DRESS IT UP!

Turkey jerky is great on its own, or served with dried cranberries and pecan halves for an extra special treat. Try serving your beef jerky with raisins and peanuts for something a little different.

Tips!

Use the leanest meat you can find. The finished product will keep longer if there's less fat. Although the jerky will last for weeks at room temperature, it's best to keep it in the fridge until your trip. That way it will keep longer on the river/lake/trail. But, be warned that it won't last long once the team gets a whiff of this smoky, tasty treat.

Jerky is a great snack on a trip. It contains a lot of protein and tastes great. I pack it in small plastic bags and hand it out in increments; otherwise it all disappears the first time people get their hands on it! I used to make this by trying to slice the turkey (or beef) into thin slices, but found that it's way easier to use ground meat. The consistent thickness means that it dries thoroughly and evenly.

- Caroline Owen

METHOD

1. Put the beef or turkey in a bowl and mix thoroughly with the mesquite seasoning.
2. Using about a baseball sized portion of meat at a time, roll out the meat between two pieces of waxed paper to about a 1/4 inch (1/2 cm).
3. Remove the top layer of waxed paper and cut into strips about 1 1/2 inches (4 cm) wide and 4 inches (10 cm) long.
4. Lift the strips off the waxed paper carefully with a spatula and place on dehydrator trays, making sure they're not touching.
5. Dry the meat according to the time suggested for your dehydrator.

Serves 12… 6… um, you better be quick or it will be gone!
30 minutes; drying time depends on your dehydrator
Effort Level: I

INGREDIENTS:
- 2 lbs (900 g) lean ground beef or turkey
- 1 4-oz pkg (110 ml) powdered mesquite seasoning

SOUPS

SOUPS While it's easy to make soup from packaged mixes, here are a few you can make from scratch.

FRENCH ONION SOUP

At home you would put this soup under the broiler for a few minutes to brown the cheese, but you won't get any complaints about this camp version.

You could start from scratch by frying fresh onions and adding water and beef bouillon cubes or use a French onion soup mix.

METHOD

1. Heat the oil and butter and brown the onions and garlic.
2. Add the maple syrup to sweeten the onions.
3. Add water, salt and pepper, beef bouillon cubes and simmer for 20 minutes.
4. Serve topped with freshly fried croutons and grated mozzarella cheese.

Short Cut!

Use a packaged French Onion Soup mix, then top with croutons and cheese.

Tips!

You can add vegetables, croutons and cheese to any soup mix.

Serves 6
15 minutes
Effort Level: I

INGREDIENTS:
- 2 onions, sliced
- 1 tbsp (15 ml) butter
- 1 tbsp (15 ml) olive oil
- 2 cloves garlic, minced
- 1 tbsp (15 ml) maple syrup
- 8 cups (2 L) water
- 2 beef bouillon cubes
- 1/2 tsp (2 ml) pepper
- 1/2 tsp (2 ml) salt
- 1 1/2 cups (375 ml) croutons
- 1 1/2 cups (375 ml) mozzarella cheese, grated

CROUTONS

Croutons are an easy way to dress up a salad or soup and a good use of leftover bread. They taste best served fresh from the pan but they can also be saved for several days.

METHOD

1. Slice the bread into 1/2 inch cubes.
2. Heat the oil in a frying pan over medium heat.
3. Add the garlic and the bread to the hot oil and stir constantly for two to four minutes. Keep the heat up but don't allow the oil to smoke.
4. Add the spices during the last minute of cooking. The bread should be browned.

Serves 6
5 minutes
Effort Level: I

INGREDIENTS:
- 3 slices bread
- 2 cloves garlic, minced
- 2 tbsp (30 ml) olive oil
- 1/2 tsp (2 ml) dried sage
- 1/2 tsp (2 ml) salt
- 1/2 tsp (2 ml) pepper

DRESS IT UP!
Add nuts like almonds or sunflower seeds to the pan and they'll toast along with the croutons.

VEGETABLE SOUP WITH COCONUT MILK

Coconut milk adds tropical flavor to this delicious soup. Because the recipe uses root vegetables that stay fresh for a long time, this soup can be made toward the end of a longer trip. The hit of vegetables will be a welcome treat!

Serves 4
30 minutes
Effort Level: II

METHOD

1. Melt butter in a large saucepan, add onion and fry until tender.
2. Add diced vegetables and fry for 3-4 minutes longer.
3. Add the marjoram, ginger, cinnamon and salt and pepper to taste, then fry over low heat for about 10 minutes.
4. Stir in the stock, almonds, chili flakes and sugar. Cover and simmer for about 15 minutes until the vegetables are tender.
5. Stir in the coconut milk powder and serve.

INGREDIENTS:
- 2 tbsp (30 ml) butter
- 1 red onion, finely chopped
- 1 cup (250 ml) turnip, diced
- 1 cup (250 ml) sweet potatoes, diced
- 1 cup (250 ml) potatoes, diced
- 1 tsp (5 ml) dried marjoram
- 1 tsp (5 ml) ginger, freshly grated
- 6 cups (1 1/2 L) stock made from bouillon cubes
- 2 tbsp (30 ml) slivered almonds
- 1 tsp (5 ml) sugar
- 1/2 tsp (2 ml) cinnamon
- 1/4 tsp (1 ml) chili flakes
- 1/2 cup (125 ml) coconut milk powder
- salt and pepper to taste

KOH SOI

Koh Soi is a traditional dish from Northern Thailand. It's a spicy coconut curry soup served over noodles with lots of vegetables that warms you from the inside out! It's quick, easy and tastes fabulous. This recipe was taught to me by a woman who owns a small restaurant in Chiang Mai, Thailand. I ate lunch there every day for a month and after a few days, she stopped asking me what I wanted to order and just brought me a bowl of Koh Soi. On my last day, I asked her to tell me the recipe, which she happily imparted with no quantities specified: a bit of this and some of that. I've experimented with it and have come up with a version that works every time.

- Caroline Owen

Serves 6
30 minutes
Effort Level: I

INGREDIENTS:
- 3 cans coconut milk
- 3 cups (750 ml) water
- 1-2 tbsp (15-30 ml) red curry paste
- 6 tbsp (90 ml) sugar
- 6 medium carrots, chopped
- 1 cup (250 ml) snow peas or sugar snap peas
- 1 block firm tofu, or 2 cups (500 ml) dried chicken pieces
- 2 cups (500 ml) bean sprouts
- 1 head medium broccoli, chopped
- 1/2 cup (125 ml) crushed roasted peanuts
- 1 cup (250 ml) dried chow mein noodles
- 3 limes
- soy sauce (to taste)
- crushed chili peppers (to taste)
- 1 package egg noodles

METHOD

1. In a large pot, boil the coconut milk, water, sugar, curry paste and chili peppers until the coconut milk starts to separate slightly (5 - 10 minutes).
2. Add the vegetables and tofu or chicken and simmer, stirring occasionally until the vegetables are softened, but not mushy.
3. In a separate pot, cook the egg noodles according to the directions on the package.
4. Line up six bowls and divide the egg noodles between the bowls, then pour a helping of soup over the noodles.
5. Top with bean sprouts, peanuts, chow mein noodles, a dash of soy sauce. Squeeze the juice of half a lime in each bowl.

DRESS IT UP!

This is a fun dish to eat with disposable wooden chopsticks. They can be used later as kindling for your next fire! Eat the solid stuff with the chopsticks and then drink the broth straight from the bowl.

Tips!

Never let on to your impressed friends that it's so easy to make! They don't need to know.

VARIATIONS!

Bean sprouts make a great topping for this soup, but only if you make it quite early in the trip - otherwise the sprouts turn to mush. Substitute a grated carrot for a sweet fresh garnish and to add a bit of crunch.

DINNER appetizers & side dishes

DINNER APPETIZERS AND SIDE DISHES

Appetizers aren't always necessary, but they are always appreciated. Some of these recipes are very fast to whip up but still look and taste impressive, especially in the context of a camping trip when you're supposed to be roughing it!

Pasta and rice are both frequent and ideal side dishes; quick to prepare, a nutritious source of carbohydrates and they go well with just about everything. We've included some tips on how to cook those basics and provided a few more adventurous side dishes for when you have the time to do a little more.

QUESADILLAS

It doesn't take long to make quesadillas and they are a delicious, warm appetizer for any day, or a Mexican-themed dinner.

Serves 6 (as appetizers)
10 minutes
Effort Level: I

INGREDIENTS:
- 8-10 small flour tortillas
- 1 tub (250 g) plain cream cheese
- 1 cup (250 ml) salsa
- 9 oz (250 g) grated cheddar cheese
- 9 oz (250 g) grated mozzarella cheese

METHOD
1. Divide the number of tortillas into pairs. On one of each pair, spread a thin layer of cream cheese.
2. On top of the cream cheese, spread a thin layer of salsa and sprinkle grated cheese.
3. Put the second of the pair on top to close it like a sandwich.
4. Using an ungreased griddle, cook each side over medium heat until the tortilla is browned and the cheese melted.
5. Cut them into wedges on a plate or cutting board.

DRESS IT UP!
Add a dollop of sour cream or plain yogurt and fresh guacamole. Sprigs of cilantro add a terrific flavor.

CREAMY CUCUMBER ROUNDS

Serves 6
10 minutes
Effort Level: I

INGREDIENTS:
- 1 box rice or other crackers
- 1 cucumber, sliced
- 1 camembert cheese, thinly wedged
- 10 oz (300 g) smoked salmon, sliced
- chopped fresh dill, to taste
- 1 lemon, zested

METHOD
1. Put a slice of cucumber on each cracker. Top with a little slice of smoked salmon and a wedge of camembert. Sprinkle with dill and lemon zest.

DRESS IT UP!
Arrange on a serving platter with some extra sprigs of dill and leaves of baby spinach.

SUSHI

With some minor trip packing limitations, this sushi recipe may not be just like Japan but it is still a wonderful treat for the palate! Sushi is an ideal appetizer (or even full meal) for an easier day when there's plenty of time to make dinner. Because sushi is lighter fare, it also gives you a great opportunity to follow it up with a rich dessert.

You can further impress by using the right names for what you are serving:

Sushi - a ball of rice seasoned with vinegar, sugar and salt
Sashimi - uncooked fish
Maki - a roll of sushi, probably the most common type
Nigiri - a rice ball with a piece of sashimi or egg on the outside
Temaki - a cone-shaped nori with the rice stuffed inside

- Jen Buck and Judy Condliffe

METHOD

1. If possible, soak the rice prior to cooking it for up to 6 hours - easy enough if it's a rest day. This will shorten cooking time, improve texture and save fuel.
2. Bring rice and water to a boil. Boil for one minute and then simmer for 20 minutes if it hasn't been soaked; for less time if it has.
3. When the rice is done simmering, take it off the heat and set aside for 10 minutes. In the meantime you can prepare your "sushi vinegar" by heating the vinegar with the white sugar and salt until dissolved. Now stir in the sushi vinegar.
4. While the rice is simmering prepare your fillings (see variations below).
5. Assemble your maki, nigiri and sashimi, and then serve with soy sauce, pickled ginger and wasabi!

Serves 6
45 minutes
Effort Level: III

INGREDIENTS:
- 2 pkgs (50 g) nori (seaweed)
- 3 cups (750 ml) sushi rice or short grained white rice
- 3 cups (750 ml) water
- 1/3 cup (80 ml) rice vinegar
- 2 tsp (10 ml) white sugar
- 1 tsp (5 ml) salt
- soy sauce to taste
- wasabi paste to taste
- pickled ginger to taste
- fillings and toppings (see variations below)

METHOD

1. Slice the carrots, avocado, cucumber and pepper in thin strips.
2. Brush sheets of nori lightly with water. You can do this with your fingers. If you use too much water, the nori will get soggy and curl; the point is to soften it very slightly so that it will not crack when you try to roll it.
3. Use about 1/2 cup (125 ml) of rice per sheet of nori. Spread the rice over the nori, leaving 1 inch (2 1/2 cm) of uncovered nori at one side.
4. Place a slice or two of smoked salmon on the rice near the rice-bordered end. It does not have to cover all the rice. Place a few strips of vegetables on the salmon. I recommend a maximum of three ingredients in each roll.
5. Roll from rice side towards uncovered side - keeping roll as tight as possible (like rolling a sleeping bag).
6. Cut into 6-8 even pieces and serve.

Variation: *Egg (Tamago) – Nigiri*

METHOD

1. Combine all ingredients to make a firm omelet.
2. Cut the omelet into 1 by 2 inch (2 1/2 by 5 cm) strips.
3. Make little oblong balls of rice and cut nori into long, 1/4 inch (1 cm) wide strips.
4. Place a piece of tamago on the rice ball, attaching it all together with a little belt of nori.

Variation: *Tuna Rolls – Tamaki (See Side Bar)*

Raw Fish (Sashimi)

Have you ever had so many fresh char you just couldn't think of enough ways to keep it exciting to eat? Right, well, if you are ever on the Coppermine or Hood Rivers you just might find yourself in such a predicament. Serving a barrel-lid piled high with hand rolls, maki and nigiri is a sure-fire crowd pleaser!

Never use old or fresh water fish for your sushi. If you don't have super fresh saltwater fish, stick with vegetarian or cooked-fish sushi.

Of course, eating raw fish is done at your own risk.

DRESS IT UP!

Sprinkle toasted sesame seeds over the sushi. Use a small vessel to serve soy sauce and wasabi. To really complete the experience, serve with miso soup. You can buy miso soup packets, powder or cubes. Wasabi peas, available at most bulk food stores, make a great snack on the side. To really take it to the next level, bring out a bottle of sake!

Tips!

Use your sleeping bag rolling technique when rolling maki. Keep it nice and tight to pack down the rice and make the structure hold – just don't squash the rice too hard or it will become a glutinous ball that can be a choking hazard!

The rice sticks less if your hands and knives are dipped in vinegar between rolls and cuts. The nori sticks together if you put a little dab of vinegar on it where you want it to attach.

Packing the nori is your biggest challenge, but one that is easily overcome. Line your food barrel with nori or place it along the back of your food pack so that it is safely tucked up against a wall and it should survive just fine!

INGREDIENTS (MAKI):
- 20 oz (600 g) smoked salmon
- 3 carrots
- 1 avocado
- 1 cucumber
- 1 green or red pepper
- rice and nori as prepared above

INGREDIENTS (NIGIRI):
- 3/4 cup (175 ml) egg powder
- 2/3 cup (150 ml) water
- 2 tbsp (30 ml) soy sauce
- 1 tsp (5 ml) sugar (optional)

INGREDIENTS (TAMAKI):
- 13 oz can (120 g) tuna
- 3 green onions, sliced
- 1/3 pkg (85 g) cream cheese

SMOKED SALMON PINWHEELS

Serves 6
10 minutes
Effort Level: I

INGREDIENTS:
- 3 flour tortillas
- 9 oz (250 g) smoked salmon
- 9 oz (250 g) cream cheese
- 1/2 red onion, thinly sliced
- 3 1/2 oz (100 g) capers
- 1/2 tsp (2 ml) black pepper

You can do almost anything with smoked salmon and it will taste upscale. This recipe delivers a classic combination but serves it a little differently. It's a quick way to prepare a tray full of tasty treats and make a small bit of salmon go a long way. With smoked salmon more is always better but whatever the quantity of your ingredients, making it this way ensures that everyone will get a taste.

METHOD
1. Spread a thin layer of cream cheese on the tortillas.
2. Place very thinly sliced onion and capers on the cream cheese, and then put slices of smoked salmon on top.
3. Spread the rest of the cream cheese over the salmon.
4. Roll the tortillas, cut into 1/2 inch (1 cm) slices and serve.

FRENCH FRIES

Serves 6
60 minutes
Effort Level: III

INGREDIENTS:
- 3 potatoes
- 1 sweet potato
- ketchup to taste
- salt to taste

This makes a good simple side dish for a slower, lounge-around-the-kitchen meal.

METHOD
1. Slice the potatoes and sweet potatoes into thin chips about 1/8 inch (3 mm) thick. If possible, dry the excess moisture from the potatoes before frying.
2. Deep fry until golden brown. Serve immediately with ketchup, cider vinegar, salt, pepper and Tabasco.

VARIATIONS!
Sprinkle cheese curds or grated cheese on top and then smother with gravy to make the French-Canadian classic, poutine!

GRAINS AND LEGUMES
COOKING CHARTS

It is easy to prepare good, wholesome meals with whole grains and legumes as the centerpiece of the meal. Grains and legumes are easy to pack and have a lot of nutritional value. Use the charts below as a quick reference when packing for your trip. You can photocopy them and tape them inside your food barrel so they are always handy.

COOKING GRAINS Here are the basic directions for cooking any grain.

1. Measure the grain and water.
2. Cover the pot and bring to a boil over high heat.
3. Turn the heat down to low and simmer for the recommended cooking time.
4. Lift the lid and test grains for tenderness.
5. If the grains need more cooking time and all the water has been absorbed, add up to 1/4 cup (60 ml) more of water, cover and continue heating.
6. When tender, remove from heat and allow the grains to sit for 5 to 10 minutes before fluffing with a fork and serving.

GRAIN	WATER	COOK TIME	APPROXIMATE YIELD
(1 cup or 250 ml dry)		(in minutes)	
Barley, pearled	3 cups (750 ml)	50-60	2 1/2 cups (625 ml)
Barley, hulled	3 cups (750 ml)	50-60	3 1/2 cups (875 ml)
Cornmeal (fine grind)	4 1/2 cups (1.1 L)	8-10	2 1/2 cups (625 ml)
Cornmeal (coarse for polenta)	4 1/2 cups (1.1 L)	8-10	2 1/2 cups (625 ml)
Millet, hulled	4 cups (1 L)	20-25	3 1/2 cups (875 ml)
Quinoa	2 cups (500 ml)	15-20	3 cups (750 ml)
Rice, white basmati	2 cups (500 ml)	15-20	3 cups (750 ml)
Rice, brown basmati	2 1/2 cups (625 ml)	35-40	3 cups (750 ml)
Rice, brown long grain	2 1/2 cups (625 ml)	45-55	3 cups (750 ml)
Rice, wild	3 cups (750 ml)	50-60	4 cups (1 L)
Couscous	1 cup (250 ml)	5	2 cups (500 ml)
Bulgur	2 cups (500 ml)	15	2 1/2 cups (625 ml)
Rolled Oats	2 cups (500 ml)	15	2 1/2 cups (625 ml)
Red River Cereal	3 cups (750 ml)	10	3 cups (750 ml)
Cream of Wheat	4 cups (1 L)	5	2 cups (500 ml)

COOKING LEGUMES To save on fuel, improve the texture of the beans and remove some of the properties that result in intestinal gas, it is wise to soak your beans and legumes for a minimum of 4 hours before you cook them. Simply cover the beans or legumes with water and let them sit. You may have to add more water as it gets absorbed.

Boiling beans and legumes can be hard on the fuel supply. Therefore it is best to cook your bean and legume-based meals over a fire when you can.

Begin by washing beans or legumes and discarding any that are discolored or badly formed. Remove debris that may be present, like small rocks and twigs. Soak the beans in water overnight. Rinse the beans or legumes with fresh water after you soak them. Never add salt to boiling beans or legumes because it will toughen the skin. Instead, season after the beans

or legumes are tender.

If cooking time is limited you can speed up the process of soaking by bringing the beans or legumes to a boil for 10 minutes. Remove the pot from the heat and drain the water. Rinse the beans, cover them with fresh water and soak for an hour.

Here are the basic directions for cooking any bean or legume.
1. Soak beans and then drain.
2. Measure the beans and water.
3. Cover the pot and bring to a boil over high heat.
4. Turn the heat down to low and simmer for the recommended cooking time.
5. Lift the lid and test beans for tenderness. If they are not yet cooked, simmer them a little longer. Add more water if required.
6. When tender, drain and serve.

BEAN OR LEGUME	WATER	COOK TIME	APPROXIMATE YIELD
(1 cup or 250 ml dry)		(in minutes)	
Adzuki	4 cups (1 L)	45-55	3 cups (750 ml)
Black Beans	2 1/2 (625 ml)	45-55	2 1/2 cups (625 ml)
Black-eyed peas	3 cups (750 ml)	60	2 1/2 cups (625 ml)
Cannellini (White Kidney Beans)	3 cups (750 ml)	45	2 1/2 cups (625 ml)
Garbanzo Beans (Chickpeas)	4 cups (1 L)	1 to 3 hours	2 cups (500 ml)
Green Split Peas	4 cups (1 L)	45	2 cups (500 ml)
Yellow Split Peas	4 cups (1 L)	75	2 cups (500 ml)
Kidney Beans	3 cups (750 ml)	60	2 1/2 cups (625 ml)
Lentils, brown	2 1/2 (625 ml)	45	2 1/2 cups (625 ml)
Lentils, green	2 cups (500 ml)	30-45	2 cups (500 ml)
Lentils, red	3 cups (750 ml)	20-30	2 1/2 cups (625 ml)
Navy Beans	3 cups (750 ml)	45-60	3 cups (750 ml)
Pinto Beans	3 cups (750 ml)	90	3 cups (750 ml)

STEAMED RICE

Rice appears on most trip menus because it goes well with most main courses, it packs well and it cooks easily. As a general rule, you can budget about 1/3 to 1/2 cup (80 to 125 ml) of dry rice per person for a meal. We recommend basmati or long grain rice. Rice is a good source of carbohydrates, and like other grains it becomes a more complete protein when combined with milk or legumes. You need a pot with a tight-fitting lid to make good rice.

METHOD

1. Put all the ingredients in a pot and bring it to a boil. If you like, you can add spice or a touch of flavored oil after it has boiled.
2. Do not stir the rice. Cover with a tight lid and put on low heat for 20 minutes - still no stirring. If you're cooking with a fire, you can set it beside the fire and take it on and off the coals occasionally to maintain the equivalent of a low heat setting. After 20 minutes you can take it off the heat, but leave the lid on until it is ready to serve.
3. Just before serving, fluff up the rice with a fork.

DRESS IT UP!
A little parsley or other herbs that are complementary to the rest of the meal will dress up plain rice.

Tips!

To make more or less rice than what is specified in this recipe, simply use a little more than twice as much cold water as rice, then add appropriate amounts of oil and salt.

Never stir or take off the lid until it is finished - really.

Leftover rice keeps well and tastes good the next day. If you have leftovers, let them cool then pack them in a plastic bag. You can add it to the eggs the next morning or serve it on its own for lunch as a side dish with a little soy sauce, hot sauce or vinaigrette dressing.

You can also reheat leftovers with milk, sugar, vanilla and raisins for rice pudding. (Take care to not boil the milk or it will scald and burn.) For real rice pudding, mix a little egg in with the milk and bake!

Serves 6
30 minutes
Effort Level: II

INGREDIENTS:
- 2 1/2 cups (550 ml) rice
- 5 cups (1125 ml) water
- 1 tsp (5 ml) flavored oil
- 1/2 tsp (2 ml) salt

PASTA

Serves 6
30 minutes for dry pasta,
10 minutes for fresh pasta
Effort Level: I

INGREDIENTS:
- 3 1/2 oz per person (100 g per person) dry pasta
- 5 oz per person (150 g per person) fresh pasta
- salt

This one is easy.

METHOD

1. Make pasta just as you would at home: cook pasta in boiled salted water until noodles are *al dente*.
2. When the pasta is cooked, drain the water from the pot using a lid and leather gloves. You should drain the water into your designated gray water area. Dilute the area later with another bucket of water.

DRESS IT UP!
Along with the sauce, Parmesan, ground pepper and parsley are all nice garnishes for pasta especially if they are fresh.

Tips!
If you're serving the pasta cold, pour some filtered water into the pot and drain it again to get rid of the extra starch and then add 1 tbsp (15 ml) of oil to prevent sticking.

CABBAGE SALAD

Serves 6
10 minutes
Effort Level: I

INGREDIENTS:
- 1/3 medium/large cabbage, red or green
- 1 carrot, grated or sliced
- 1 green pepper, diced

It's not easy to have salad on a camping trip, especially on longer adventures, because typical salad ingredients won't last very long or are too fragile. However, here are a few tasty recipes that can be easily made in a camp kitchen and give you a refreshing bit of crunch!

With just a little attention and by removing browning leaves, a cabbage can last 2 or 3 weeks in a food barrel. Unlike lettuce or more flamboyant salad greens that wither under heat and pressure, the cabbage is dependable which is perhaps why it is used as a term of endearment by the French in the expression *mon petit chou*, or "my little cabbage".

A medium to large cabbage will make three or four salads for a group of six.

METHOD

1. Wash and remove the browned parts of outer leaves and then chop the cabbage.
2. Combine with carrots and green pepper.
3. Top with dressing of your choice.

DRESS IT UP!
This can be served separately but it is hardy enough to rub shoulders with warm food.

VARIATIONS!
Add a 1/4 cup (60 ml) of raisins for a sweet-savory salad.

SCALLOPED POTATOES

This can be a side dish or you can add cheese, veggies and ham and serve it as the main course. This recipe comes from my mother's kitchen. We used to fight for the thickened crust on top. You can use fresh or dehydrated potatoes. There are also scalloped potato prepared mixes available from the grocery store.

- Mark Scriver

METHOD

1. Heat the briquettes for the Dutch oven or get your oven ready to bake at 350°F (175°C).
2. Slice the potatoes and onion into 1/8 inch (3 mm) slices.
3. Combine the flour, salt and pepper. Put a thin layer of potatoes and onion on the bottom of the baking pan or Dutch oven.
4. Sprinkle a spoonful of flour mixture over the potatoes. Alternate layers of potatoes, onions and the flour mixture.
5. Add milk until the liquid is a half inch below the surface of the potatoes.
6. Spread the butter around the edge of the pan. It will mix throughout the dish as it cooks but will also prevent the milk from climbing the edge of the pot and boiling over. The flour, butter and milk combine to make a thick creamy sauce. Bake in the Dutch oven for one hour.

VARIATIONS!

For a complete meal, you can add broccoli and cauliflower (which taste good in a thickened milk sauce) as well as cooked ham. You can also sprinkle a bit of cheddar or gruyere cheese on top, which allows you to reduce the amount of butter because of the oil in the cheese.

Short Cut!

Use rehydrated potatoes to reduce the cooking time and save the weight and bulk of fresh potatoes.

Serves 6
60 minutes
Effort Level: II

INGREDIENTS:
- 8 medium potatoes
- 1 onion
- 3 cups (750 ml) milk, made from powder
- 3 tbsp (45 ml) butter or margarine
- 1/2 cup (125 ml) all purpose flour
- 1 tsp (5 ml) salt
- 1 tsp (5 ml) pepper

GRILLED PESTO PORTOBELLO MUSHROOMS

This versatile recipe can be served as a side dish, an appetizer, or even be dressed up as a main course! It's a perfect option for vegetarians in the group when meat is being grilled for the omnivores. Just serve it on top of a toasted and buttered half of multigrain roll.

METHOD
1. Cut the stems off the mushrooms.
2. Spread the underside of the mushroom caps lightly with pesto and top with sliced cheese.
3. Grill on a greased barbeque or grate over medium heat until the cheese is melted and the mushrooms are warmed through.

Serves 6
15 minutes
Effort Level: I

INGREDIENTS:
- 6 portobello mushrooms
- 10 oz jar (300 ml) pesto sauce
- 6 slices (170 g) provolone or mozzarella cheese, sliced

LEFT Grilled Portobello Mushrooms on the portable Cobb Premier BBQ.

GRILLED VEGETABLES

If you have space on the grill you can cook onion slices, green and red pepper, asparagus, broccoli or other vegetables, with or without skewers. The marinade and grilling sauce will prevent the vegetables from drying out as they cook.

Serves 6
30 minutes
Effort Level: II

INGREDIENTS:
- 1/2 cup (125 ml) olive oil
- 1 tbsp (15 ml) balsamic vinegar
- 2 cloves garlic, crushed
- 1 tsp (5 ml) Dijon mustard
- 1 tsp (5 ml) dried oregano
- 1 tsp (5 ml) dried basil
- 1/4 tsp (1 ml) pepper
- 1 small eggplant, cubed
- 2 large carrots, sliced
- 6 new potatoes, halved
- 1 zucchini, sliced
- 1 red pepper,
  chopped 1 inch squares
- 1 green pepper,
  chopped 1 inch squares
- 1 yellow pepper,
  chopped 1 inch squares
- 1 large onion, wedged

METHOD
1. Prepare the marinade by combining the oil, vinegar, garlic, mustard and spices in a large stainless steel bowl. Toss in the zucchini, peppers and onion.
2. In a pot of boiling water, cook the potatoes for 10 minutes or until slightly tender. After 5 minutes, add the carrots (so that they cook for 5 minutes); after 7 minutes add the eggplant, (so it cooks for 3 minutes).
3. Drain the pot and add the potatoes, carrots and eggplant to the marinade.
4. Put all vegetables on skewers, and then grill over medium heat until they are cooked through. You can occasionally baste the vegetables with more of the grilling sauce but do this sparingly or it will slow the cooking process.

Tips!
It is easier to grill if you load each skewer with vegetables that will take about the same time to cook.

Serve this with fresh grilled fish and a mix of wild and brown rice!

SESAME VINAIGRETTE

An oil and vinegar dressing or vinaigrette is the simplest dressing to make for a salad and allows for a lot of variations. This is a multi-use dressing or sauce that can be used on a range of dishes including salad and rice.

METHOD

1. You can just mix everything together at once but if you have time, the longer the spices sit in the oil, the more their flavors will release and mix. Stir and pour on the salad just before serving.

DRESS IT UP!
Toasted sesame seeds sprinkled on a salad go really well with this dressing.

VARIATIONS!
There is no end of flavor combinations you can use. Bring a small variety of good quality oils and vinegars in small containers so you can experiment. Try olive oil and lemon or lime juice or vinegar and add 1/4 cup (60 ml) of crumbled blue cheese. Some dressings will taste great with a dash of Worcestershire or Tabasco sauce. Use spices that you know go well together, keep a ratio of 3 or 4:1 for oil: vinegar and let your creativity take over!

Serves 6
5 minutes
Effort Level: I

INGREDIENTS:
- 1/2 cup (125 ml) olive oil
- 1/4 cup (60 ml) sesame oil
- 1/4 cup (60 ml) white balsamic vinegar
- 1/2 tsp (2 ml) salt
- 1/2 tsp (2 ml) pepper
- 1 tbsp (15 ml) Dijon mustard or 1 tsp (5 ml) dry mustard
- 1 tsp (5 ml) garlic, minced
- 1 tsp (5 ml) maple syrup

DINNER main dishes

DINNER MAIN DISHES Ahh! The main course.
If you have any room in your belly after eating all those appetizers and soups, here are some main courses to satisfy the
whole group.

CHICKEN AND CASHEW STIR-FRY

Black bean sauce can be found at Asian food stores and it is the secret ingredient for this yummy stir-fry. Pack it in a leak-proof bottle.

DRESS IT UP!

Make it an Asian-themed night. Bring along chopsticks for everyone to use, serve with hot sauces, and finish the meal with fortune cookies!

Tips!

If you want to thicken the juices to a sauce, dissolve 2 or 3 tbsp (30 to 45 ml) of cornstarch or flour completely in 1/4 cup (60 ml) of cold water and add it to the wok when everything is almost done cooking. Bring to a boil and then simmer 3 or 4 minutes until it thickens and the starchy taste disappears.

VARIATIONS!

Stir-fries are one of the most versatile dinners. Try cubed beef, potatoes, a beef broth cube and a bit of wine for a beef stew, or ham with maple syrup, Dijon mustard and pineapple.

METHOD

1. If using dehydrated chicken follow the rehydration instructions. If using fresh chicken, cut into strips. If using tofu, cube.
2. In a small bowl, combine soy sauce, black bean sauce, sugar, sesame oil and 2 tbsp (30 ml) of water. Add cornstarch and mix until smooth.
3. Heat vegetable oil in a wok and stir-fry chicken or tofu until browned and cooked through. Remove chicken or tofu from the pan and reserve.
4. Heat more vegetable oil and add garlic, ginger, onion slices and chili flakes and stir-fry until onions are soft.
5. Add vegetables and stir-fry for one minute.
6. Add sauce and stir-fry until vegetables are cooked.
7. Add chicken or tofu and mix well.
8. Serve into bowls over rice and sprinkle with cashews. Provide extra soy sauce.

Serves 6
45 minutes
Effort Level: II

INGREDIENTS:
- 3 large chicken breasts or equivalent in dehydrated chicken or tofu
- 4 tbsp (60 ml) soy sauce
- 4 tbsp (60 ml) black bean sauce
- 1 tbsp (15 ml) sugar
- 2 tsp (10 ml) sesame oil
- 1/4 cup (60 ml) water
- 1 tsp (5 ml) cornstarch
- 1/3 cup (80 ml) vegetable oil
- 2 cloves garlic, minced
- 1 tbsp (15 ml) ginger, freshly chopped
- 1 large onion, sliced
- 1/2 tsp (2 ml) chili flakes
- 3 cups (750 ml) mixed vegetables
- 1/2 cup (125 ml) cashews

SPICY THAI PEANUT TOFU

Serves 6
30 minutes
Effort Level: IV

INGREDIENTS:
- 1 cup (250 ml) smooth peanut butter
- 1/4 cup (50 ml) soy sauce
- 4 tbsp (60 ml) vegetable or peanut oil
- 2 cloves garlic, minced
- 1 tbsp (15 ml) ginger, chopped fresh
- 1 tsp (5 ml) chili flakes
- 1 large onion, diced
- 2 pkgs (680 g) extra firm tofu, cubed
- 1 pkg (454 g) rice noodles
- 1/2 cup (125 ml) peanuts, chopped

METHOD

1. Boil a large pot of water and remove from heat.
2. Place noodles in the water and soak until they are soft (about 5 minutes), then drain water and reserve the noodles.
3. Whisk peanut butter and soy sauce together until smooth.
4. Heat 1 tbsp (15 ml) oil in a wok.
5. Add garlic, fresh ginger and chili flakes, then stir-fry for one minute.
6. Add onion and stir-fry until soft.
7. Add 1 tbsp (15 ml) of oil and toss in the tofu. Stir-fry tofu until it is browned on all sides. Stir frequently to prevent sticking.
8. Add the peanut butter sauce with the tofu mixture and cook until peanut butter and soy sauce coats the tofu.
9. Serve over the rice noodles and garnish with chopped peanuts.

CHICK'N'RICE

This creamy dish is a nice way to serve fresh chicken early on the trip.

METHOD

1. In a wok, sauté the onion and garlic in the oil until they are translucent.
2. Add the chicken and cook it until the outside is browned.
3. Add the carrots, sauté until tender and then add the mushrooms.
4. Stir the mushroom soup mix with milk and add it to the wok along with the dried peas, corn and dried chicken.
5. Simmer for about 15 minutes, or until everything is hot and bubbling. You can add extra milk if the sauce gets too thick. Season to taste with salt and pepper.

Serves 6
30 minutes
Effort Level: I

INGREDIENTS:
- 2 tbsp (30 ml) vegetable oil
- 2 cloves garlic, crushed
- 1 onion, diced
- 3 carrots, sliced
- 20 mushrooms or equivalent dried
- 1/2 cup (125 ml) dried peas
- 1/2 cup (125 ml) dried corn
- 3 fresh or dried chicken breasts or equivalent amount of tofu, cubed
- 1 pkg (110 g) cream of mushroom soup base
- 2 cups (500 ml) milk, made from powder
- 3 cups (750 ml) cooked basmati rice
- salt and pepper to taste

WILD MUSHROOM RISOTTO

To stir or not to stir is the great debate when it comes to risotto; some believe risotto should be a workout for your forearm, while others think it should be an exercise in minimalism. When cooking on a testy camp stove with limited simmering capabilities or over a fire, stirring constantly and paying attention is the only way to go.

The goal is to end up with a creamy, filling and delicious meal that will warm your belly after a big day. I served this meal to a group of down trodden hikers on the Appalachian Trail. There was a wonderful, satisfied silence as they all snuggled in under our shelter and let the comfort of a rich meal take away the chill of a rainy day.

Note that risotto rice has more starch than other types of rice and is what makes risotto creamy. You can get many kinds of risotto rice but the most common type is Arborio.

- Joanna Baker

DRESS IT UP!
Use good quality, freshly grated parmesan cheese, like parmigiano reggiano. Garnish the risotto with toasted pine nuts, lemon zest or fresh parsley.

Serves 6
30 minutes
Effort Level: IV

INGREDIENTS:
- 7 cups (1.75 L) water
- 2 cubes vegetable bouillon cubes
- 1/2 cup (125 ml) dried mushrooms
- 3 tbsp (45 ml) olive oil
- 1 onion, diced
- 2 cloves garlic, minced
- 2 cups (500 ml) risotto rice
- 1/2 cup (125 ml) parmesan cheese, grated
- 1 tbsp (15 ml) margarine
- 1 cup (250 ml) white wine (optional)

METHOD
1. Bring water to a boil in a medium pot.
2. Add bouillon cubes and remove from heat.
3. Remove one cup of the broth and pour it into a small bowl, then add the mushrooms to rehydrate them and cover.
4. Cover the pot of broth to keep the contents warm.
5. In another pot, heat olive oil and add onions. Cook onions until they are pale gold, then add garlic and cook for one more minute. Be careful not to burn the garlic.
6. Add rice and stir to coat with oil. Add the wine, if using. Stir until most of the wine has been cooked off or absorbed.
7. Reduce heat to lowest possible and add one cup of stock.
8. Stir until all of the stock has been absorbed. Add one cup of stock at a time and stir frequently until all the stock is absorbed.

9. When you have added most of the stock and the rice is tender, add the mushrooms and the liquid they were soaking in. Cook until all the liquid has been absorbed.
10. Remove the pot from heat. Add most of the parmesan cheese, all of the butter and season with salt and pepper.
11. Serve with the remaining parmesan sprinkled on top.

GOOD OL' TUNA MAC AND CHEESE

Tips!

You can add any dried veggies that you like to the pot of noodles when it is cooking: broccoli, cauliflower, corn etc!

VEGETARIAN OPTION
Omit the tuna.

Macaroni and cheese is the ultimate comfort food: easy and quick to prepare, easy to clean up and perfect for a rainy or cold day.

METHOD

1. Bring a large pot of water to a boil and cook the macaroni for about 10 minutes.
2. Add the dried peas and green beans and cook for another 5 minutes.
3. Drain macaroni, peas and beans and keep warm in large pot.
4. Meanwhile, in a frying pan or wok, sauté the onions in oil until translucent.
5. Add the carrots to the pan and cook until they start to soften.
6. Add the sautéed onions and carrots to the large pot and stir over low heat. Add tuna, cheddar powder, milk, grated cheese and pepper. Stir well after each ingredient has been added.

Serves 6
20 minutes
Effort Level: I
Vegetarian Option

INGREDIENTS:
- 1 tbsp (15 ml) canola oil
- 1 onion, diced
- 2 carrots, sliced
- 4 cups (1 L) tri-color or whole wheat macaroni
- 1/2 cup (125 ml) freeze-dried peas
- 1/2 cup (125 ml) freeze-dried beans
- 3 cans (360 g) tuna, drained, or dried and rehydrated
- 1/2 cup (125 ml) cheddar cheese powder
- 2 cups (500 ml) skim milk, made from powder
- 7 oz (200 g) cheddar, grated

ITALIAN ORZO

Orzo has a great texture when cooked. This recipe is a nice change from the typical pasta dish.

Serves 6
30-40 minutes
Effort Level: I

INGREDIENTS:
- 3 cups (750 ml) orzo
- 1 tbsp (15 ml) olive oil
- 1 onion, chopped
- 2 cloves garlic, crushed
- 1 zucchini or broccoli, diced, or 1 cup dried and rehydrated
- 1/2 cup (125 ml) red pepper, diced, or 1/2 cup dried and rehydrated
- 1/2 cup (125 ml) green pepper, diced, or 1/2 cup dried and rehydrated
- 1/4 tsp (1 ml) chili flakes
- 2 tsp (10 ml) dried oregano
- 2 tsp (10 ml) dried basil
- 28 oz can (796 ml) diced tomatoes, or 1 cup dried tomato powder, rehydrated
- 2 cans (240 g) tuna, drained, or dried and rehydrated
- small can (280 g) sliced black olives, drained
- 1 cup (250 ml) parmesan cheese, grated

METHOD
1. Cook the orzo in boiling water until *al dente* and then drain.
2. In a wok, heat the oil and sauté the garlic and onion until translucent.
3. If you are using fresh vegetables, add the broccoli, zucchini and peppers. (If you are using dehydrated vegetables, add them later.)
4. Add the canned tomato or rehydrated tomato powder.
5. Allow the sauce to heat up again and add the dried broccoli, zucchini and peppers along with the basil, oregano and chili pepper flakes.
6. Simmer for 5 minutes, then reduce the heat and stir in the orzo, tuna and olives. Simmer for a few more minutes.
7. Stir in half of the parmesan and save half to garnish each dish.

PESTO PINE
NUT FUSILLI

Serves 6
30 minutes
Effort Level: II

INGREDIENTS:
- 18 oz (500 g) tri-color fusilli
- 3 tbsp (45 ml) olive oil
- 1 clove garlic, crushed
- 1 onion, chopped
- 2 carrots, diced
- 1 cup (250 ml) sun-dried
  tomatoes, chopped
- 1 green pepper, chopped
- 1 red pepper, chopped
- 1 cup (250 ml) pine nuts, toasted
- 10 oz jar (300 ml) pesto or equivalent dried pesto-parmesan mix
- 1/2 cup (125 ml) parmesan, grated

METHOD
1. Cook the noodles until they are *al dente*.
2. In a wok, sauté onion and garlic in olive oil until translucent.
3. Add the diced carrots and cook for 3 to 5 minutes.
4. Add the sun-dried tomatoes and peppers, and cook for another 5 minutes.
5. Add the cooked and drained noodles and toss.
6. Add a jar of pesto (or dried pesto mix), and toss until coated.
7. Add the toasted pine nuts and toss.
8. Serve topped with grated parmesan.

PASTA PAELLA

This is a great meal with a unique taste. It's easy to make, colorful and delicious. It's a favorite both on the trail and at home.

- Wendy Grater

METHOD

1. In a wok, sauté the onions, garlic, red peppers and chili in oil.
2. Add chicken (and shrimp if using raw), and cook until warm.
3. Add the tomatoes, chicken broth, hot water and reserved clam juice and then add the pepper, saffron and oregano.
4. Bring it to a boil and add the orzo. Cover and simmer for 15 minutes.
5. Add the clams, shrimp (if canned) and peas.
6. Simmer for 10 minutes and serve.

DRESS IT UP!
Serve this with a green salad and fresh-baked biscuits.

VARIATIONS!
To make it a pesco-vegetarian dish, substitute dried chicken with soy chunks and use vegetarian bouillon cubes.

Serves 6
30 minutes
Effort Level: II

INGREDIENTS:
- 1 tbsp (15 ml) olive oil
- 1 onion, chopped
- 1 clove garlic, minced
- 1 red pepper, diced
- 1/2 tsp (2 ml) chili flakes
- 2 chicken breasts, cubed, or one cup dried chicken, rehydrated
- 5 oz can (142 g) baby clams, reserve juice
- 2.5 oz can (70 g) shrimp, or 24 raw fresh shrimp, deveined and shelled, or dried
- 28 oz can (796 ml) diced tomatoes, or 2 cups dried tomatoes
- 1 cup (250 ml) chicken broth made from bouillon cubes
- 1 cup (250 ml) hot water
- 1 cup (250 ml) freeze-dried peas
- 2 cups (500 ml) orzo noodles
- 1/4 tsp (1 ml) saffron
- 1/4 tsp (1 ml) oregano
- 1/4 tsp (1 ml) black pepper

BÉCHAMEL SAUCE OR CHEESE SAUCE

Makes 1 1/2 cups (375ml)

10 minutes

Effort Level: II

INGREDIENTS:
- 3 tbsp (45 ml) butter, margarine or olive oil
- 3 tbsp (45 ml) all purpose white flour
- 1 1/2 cups (375 ml) milk, made from powder
- 18 oz (500 g), grated emmenthal cheese

This is a very versatile recipe and entire careers have been dedicated to its perfection. It is great over vegetables, can thicken a stir-fry or serve as the base for a cheese sauce.

METHOD

1. Melt the butter over low heat. Oil or margarine will work too, but if you only brought a bit of butter on your trip this is a good time to use it.
2. Add the white flour and cook, stirring frequently with a wood or plastic spoon for 3 to 5 minutes over a low heat. If you don't cook the sauce long enough, it will taste starchy. Cook it too hot and it will burn and taste bitter.
3. Remove it from the heat and slowly stir in the milk. You can slightly reduce the amount of liquid for a thicker sauce.
4. Return it to the heat and whisk until the sauce becomes thick and smooth. Let it simmer a few minutes and it is ready to serve.

Cheese Sauce

To make a cheese sauce, slowly add 18 oz (500 g) of grated emmenthal cheese, stirring constantly until smooth. Stir regularly and make sure it is over low heat.

If you're adding it to a vegetable stir-fry, add it just before the vegetables are done so you can let them simmer together and let the flavors mingle.

VARIATIONS!

You can add any variety of spices just before you start whisking it, but if it turns out well, the sauce can stand alone without spices. Try a hint of nutmeg or saffron. You can add a half a beef bouillon cube to make gravy for mashed potatoes or add grated cheese to make a rich cheese sauce. However, this is wonderful over steamed or quickly fried fresh vegetables on a bed of pasta. This sauce is used in the recipe for *Smoked Salmon Linguine*.

SMOKED SALMON LINGUINI

DRESS IT UP!
Garnish with a bit of fresh dill.

This is one of my favorite meals on trips and is all about letting the ingredients impress rather than the spices.

- Mark Scriver

METHOD

1. Add the linguini and 1 tsp of oil to a large pot of boiling water and cook the pasta until it is *al dente*.
2. Prepare the béchamel sauce and add the smoked salmon.
3. Add the onions and capers. Resist the temptation to add other vegetables to this dish because they will mask the delicious and delicate flavor of the smoked salmon.
4. Serve over linguini.

Serves 6
20 minutes
Effort Level: II

INGREDIENTS:
- 11 oz (300 g) smoked salmon
- 1/2 red onion, sliced thinly
- 2 tbsp (30 ml) capers
- 18 oz (500 g) linguini
- 1 tsp (5 ml) olive oil
- 1 1/2 cups (375 ml) béchamel sauce (page 167)

MARINADE AND GRILLING SAUCE

Tips!

For chicken and red meat, sear on both sides by cooking at a high temperature for a minute or two, which will seal in the juices. Recoat with the marinade and finish cooking at a lower heat.

Try to only flip things once during cooking because the center of the food will cook better if it isn't flipped repeatedly. Fish and vegetables are more fragile and can usually be flipped only once without falling apart anyway. Repeated flipping tends to dry food out and doesn't cook it efficiently.

Be careful to keep sauce that has come in contact with raw meat away from the food in the last few minutes of cooking.

Use this grilling sauce to prevent food from drying out when you're cooking it over a fire. It will also help sear the outside of the food and retain its moisture.

The acidity of this sauce will tenderize meat. Fish or vegetables shouldn't have more than 15 minutes in this acidic bath or they will lose their texture.

METHOD

1. Mix all ingredients and marinate the raw food for 15 minutes or less before cooking.
2. Reapply the sauce sparingly during grilling.

Serves 6
5 minutes
Effort Level: I

INGREDIENTS:
- 1/3 cup (80 ml) olive oil
- 1/4 cup (60 ml) Dijon mustard
- 1/4 cup (60 ml) maple syrup
- 1/4 cup (60 ml) lemon or lime juice, or vinegar
- 2 tbsp (30 ml) onion, finely chopped
- 1 tsp (5 ml) garlic powder
- 1 tsp (5 ml) pepper
- dash hot pepper sauce

GRILLED FISH

Serves 10

30 minutes (includes the catching of the fish)

Effort Level: depends on the river or lake

INGREDIENTS:
- 4 lb (2 kg) lake trout, filleted
- 1/3 cup (80 ml) olive oil
- 1/4 cup (60 ml) Dijon mustard
- 1/4 cup (60 ml) maple syrup
- 1/4 cup (60 ml) lemon juice
- 2 tbsp (30 ml) onion, finely chopped
- 1 tsp (5 ml) garlic powder
- 1 tsp (5 ml) pepper
- dash hot pepper sauce

"We have room on the grill for four 4 lb trout. Throw everything else back." We used stoves for most of our trip down the Hood River, but in the few spots where there was abundant wood, we would build a modest fire. The anglers were back within 10 minutes and shortly after that the fish were filleted and on the grill. We had the sense not to cook much else for supper and just ate huge helpings of delicious fresh fish.

- Mark Scriver

METHOD
1. Clean the grill of the firebox well.
2. Combine all the ingredients to make a marinade and add the fillets.
3. Brush the grill with oil. Place the fillets skin side up on the grill. Turn them carefully and only once, just before they are cooked halfway through. Use two spatulas so that you can flip the fish by supporting both ends of the fillet.

DRESS IT UP!
Serve with parsley and lemon. Wild rice is a perfect match for this meal.

PAN-FRIED FISH

Fish taste best when they are cooked within hours - or minutes - of being caught. The Hood River is renowned for its lake trout and on one trip, the first boat down a particular set of rapids had caught a nice big one before the last boat had even made it through. "What should I do with him, Marko?" Joe asked with a gleam in his eye. "Lunchtime!" I said, already heading for shore. We didn't do anything fancy, but that fish and another that was caught mere minutes later were being fried up over the stove within 10 minutes.

- Mark Scriver

Serves 6
20 minutes
Effort Level: I

INGREDIENTS:
- 6 lbs (2.7 kg) fish, filleted or gutted
- 3 tbsp (45 ml) vegetable oil
- 1 tbsp (15 ml) butter or margarine
- 1/2 cup (125 ml) all purpose white flour (optional)
- 1/2 cup (125 ml) crushed crackers, cornmeal, or bread crumbs (optional)
- salt and pepper to taste
- parsley or chives (optional)

METHOD

1. If you want to use a breading, blend the flour with the crushed crackers, cornmeal or bread crumbs and dredge the fish in it. Breading will make the fish crispier and not alter the taste very much.
2. Cover the bottom of the pan with oil. Heat.
3. Add the butter and throughout cooking, keep the heat just below the point where the butter would smoke.
4. Add the fish when the oil and butter are hot. While cooking fish is pretty simple, the critical part is getting the right amount of heat and flipping the fish at the right time so that it gets cooked in the middle without getting overdone on the outside. Flip the fish over when they are not quite done half-way through.
5. Add salt and pepper just before serving.

Variation: Blackened Fillets
Dry off the fillets and dredge them in the flour and spice mixture before cooking as described above.

INGREDIENTS (BLACKENED FILLETS):
- 1/4 cup (60 ml) flour or crushed crackers
- 1 tsp (5 ml) garlic powder
- 1/4 tsp (1 ml) cayenne
- 1/2 tsp (2 ml) paprika
- 1/2 tsp (2 ml) parsley
- 1/2 tsp (2 ml) dill

Tips!

If you're cooking fillets, cook the skin side last because it will lie flat. Put the tails or the thinnest part of the fillets away from the hottest part of the pan.

If you're cooking gutted fish or very thick fillets, it will take a little more time to cook, so place a lid loosely over the pan to help the middle cook more quickly. If you put a bit of lemon juice over the fish before you put the lid on, the steam will help to cook the thickest part of the fish and avoid overcooking the outside. You want more frying than steaming, so allow the steam to escape to prevent the fish from getting soggy.

BLACK FEATHER
BURRITOS

Mexican night is always a favorite on a canoe trip. Everyone gets to assemble their own burrito to get exactly the combination of flavors they want.

DRESS IT UP!
Try a Mexican theme night. Start the meal with nachos baked in the Dutch oven, along with either virgin or real margaritas. Finish off with a few lessons in salsa dancing around the campfire!

Tips!
Despite the fact that this looks like a complicated meal, it is fast to prepare, tasty and very filling on a cool, rainy night.

METHOD

1. Cook 1 1/2 cups (375 ml) of basmati rice to produce 3 cups (750 ml) of cooked rice.
2. Heat some olive oil in the wok and sauté the onion, garlic and pepper.
3. Add two packages of dehydrated refried beans along with the tomato paste, water, and one package of taco seasoning. Heat until bubbly, stirring frequently.
4. Put the grated cheese, lettuce or cabbage, sour cream and salsa in separate bowls to serve as condiments.
5. Prepare guacamole by combining the avocados, the minced garlic, chili powder, salt and the juice from half a lemon.
6. Prepare the tortillas by heating them briefly on each side on ungreased griddle.
7. Fold up one end and roll or fold into an envelope and enjoy with a helping of cooked basmati on the side.

Serves 6
30 minutes
Effort Level: II

INGREDIENTS:
- 2 tbsp (30 ml) olive oil
- 2 cloves garlic, crushed
- 1 green pepper, diced
- 2 pkgs - 7 oz (200 g) each dehydrated refried beans
- 7 1/2 oz can (210 ml) tomato paste
- 1 cup (250 ml) water
- 1 1/4 oz pkg (35 g pkg) taco seasoning mix
- 12 tortillas
- 1/2 cup (125 ml) cheddar cheese, grated
- 1/2 cup (125 ml) mozzarella cheese, grated
- 1 cup (250 ml) lettuce or cabbage, grated
- 1 cup (250 ml) salsa
- 4-5 ripe avocados, mashed
- 1-2 cloves garlic, minced
- 1 tsp (5 ml) chili powder
- 1/2 tsp (2 ml) salt
- 1/2 lemon
- 3 cups (750 ml) cooked basmati rice

CHEESE FONDUE

Serves 6
30 minutes
Effort Level: II

INGREDIENTS:
- 1 1/4 cup (300 ml) white wine
- 1 cup (250 ml) milk, made from powder
- 26 oz (750 g) gruyere cheese, grated
- 9 oz (250 g) emmenthal cheese, grated
- 2 cloves garlic, crushed
- 1/2 tsp (2 ml) pepper
- 1/2 tsp (2 ml) nutmeg
- 3 tbsp (45 ml) cornstarch
- splash fruit brandy

INGREDIENTS:
(DIPPING SUGGESTIONS):
- 1 loaf crusty French bread
- 2 cups (500 ml) broccoli florets
- 2 cups (500 ml) cauliflower florets
- 1 red pepper, chopped
- 1 green pepper, chopped
- 1 onion, wedged
- 2 apples, chopped
- 2 cups (500 ml) cherry tomatoes
- 2 cups (500 ml) baby potatoes, cooked
- 2 cups (500 ml) ham, cooked and cubed

A family friend, Ruth Anne Boos, introduced our family to cheese fondue in Gruyere, Switzerland. Since then our Christmas Eve tradition has been to enjoy this delightful, social meal. The thing I like about it the most is that you really can't keep track of how much you've eaten. As long as you can control the heat, this is an easy meal on a trip.

- Mark Scriver

METHOD

1. Heat 1 cup (250 ml) of wine and the milk, then add the garlic, nutmeg and pepper. It will curdle.
2. Gradually add the grated gruyere and emmenthal cheese.
3. When the cheese is melting into a blob and it looks like it won't work, mix the cornstarch with another 1/4 cup (60ml) of wine and pour it in.
4. Keep it just below the boiling point, stir frequently and it will turn into a smooth, rich sauce.

DRESS IT UP!
Add an optional splash of fruit brandy or fruit liqueur.

Tips!

It is hard to guess the right quantities of things to dip, but you can fry up leftovers for breakfast. It's hard to fit more than six people around one pot, so if your group is larger than that and you make more, split it into two pots.

It's easier to make this over a stove, but I have often made it in a wok over a firebox. My final tip is that it's smart to help out with the preparation of this meal so you won't have to wash the pot.

VEGETARIAN
SPAGHETTI SAUCE

You can make this sauce before the trip using all fresh ingredients and dehydrate it, or assemble it on the trip with dried ingredients as described below.

DRESS IT UP!
Serve with garlic bread.

Tips!

For a meat sauce, add freeze-dried ground beef to the sauce instead of bulgur.

METHOD

1. In the wok, sauté the onion and garlic in oil until translucent.
2. Add the green pepper, bulgur and spices and stir until the bulgur is toasted.
3. Add the canned tomatoes and tomato paste and stir. Add the dried mushrooms, dried broccoli and brown sugar. Add water occasionally to compensate for the absorption of the bulgur and dried veggies. Simmer for about 20 minutes, or until the bulgur is soft. Add extra spicing to taste. While the sauce is cooking, heat a large pot of water to a rolling boil. Add 1 tbsp (15 ml) of oil and then add spaghetti noodles and cook until *al dente*. Drain carefully. Serve noodles and sauce with grated parmesan cheese.

Serves 6
30 minutes
Effort Level: I

INGREDIENTS:
- 2 tbsp (30 ml) olive oil
- 1 clove garlic, crushed
- 1 onion, diced
- 1 green pepper, diced
- 1/2 cup (125 ml) dried broccoli
- 1/2 cup (125 ml) bulgur
- 1 tbsp (15 ml) dried oregano
- 1 tsp (5 ml) dried basil
- 1 tbsp (15 ml) brown sugar
- 28 oz can (796 ml) crushed tomatoes
- 7 1/2 oz can (225 ml) tomato paste
- 1 cup (250 ml) dried mushrooms
- 1 cup (250 ml) parmesan cheese, grated
- 26 oz (750 g) whole wheat spaghetti noodles

DEEP DISH PIZZA

As you know, pizza can be topped with just about anything. You can make this in any type of oven, but because you won't get very many servings per pan, this meal is best suited to smaller groups. You need two 10-inch pans. To make it vegetarian, simply omit the meat.

Serves 6
60 minutes
Effort Level: I

INGREDIENTS:
- 5 cups (1,125 ml) biscuit mix
- 16 oz can (475 ml) tomato sauce, or dried and rehydrated
- 4 oz can (120 ml) tomato paste, or dried and rehydrated
- 1 tbsp (15 ml) sugar
- 24 oz (680 g) mozzarella cheese, grated
- 1/2 cup (125 ml) parmesan cheese, grated
- 2 tbsp (30 ml) olive oil
- 1 onion, sliced
- 1/2 red pepper, sliced
- 1/2 green pepper, sliced
- 6 mushrooms, sliced
- 8 oz (226 g) pepperoni, sliced
- 1/2 cup (125 ml) sliced black olives
- 1 tbsp (15 ml) oregano
- 1 tbsp (15 ml) basil
- 2 cloves garlic, minced

METHOD
1. Heat the briquettes for the Dutch oven or get your oven ready to bake at 350°F (175°C).
2. Mix the biscuit mix with water to form a firm but pliable dough.
3. Divide the dough in half and roll it out into the pans, pushing the dough up the sides to create a deep crust.
4. Sprinkle the dough with parmesan cheese.
5. Combine the tomato sauce and paste with the sugar and spread it on top of the parmesan cheese.
6. Layer the toppings and sprinkle the grated mozzarella on top.
7. Bake the pizza for 20 minutes or until the dough is cooked, the cheese is melted and the sauce is bubbling.

Short Cut!
Use a pre-made crust. These do not keep indefinitely and can be a bit fragile so check the expiry, pack it carefully, and use it in the first few days of a trip.

Tips!
To make the pizza cook faster, sauté the vegetables until slightly browned, then add the tomato sauce, paste, sugar, oregano and basil.

VARIATIONS!
You can of course use any combination of toppings and cheese or substitute a yeast dough.

ROCKIN' MOROCCAN STEW

Serves 6

40 minutes

Effort Level: II

INGREDIENTS:
- 1 cup (250 ml) vegetable broth made from bouillon
- 1/3 cup (80 ml) olive oil
- 1 onion, chopped
- 1 clove garlic, crushed
- 1 sweet potato, diced
- 1 cup (250 ml) dried green beans
- 1 red pepper, chopped
- 1/2 cup (125 ml) soy chunks
- 28 oz can (796 ml) diced tomatoes
- 1/2 tsp (2 ml) thyme
- 1/4 tsp (1 ml) ginger, ground
- 1/4 tsp (1 ml) nutmeg, ground
- 1/4 tsp (1 ml) cinnamon, ground
- 3 cloves
- pinch chili flakes
- 1/2 cup (125 ml) prunes, pitted and halved
- 1/3 cup (80 ml) dried apricots, diced
- 8 oz can (250 ml) artichoke hearts, reserve juice
- 1/2 cup (125 ml black olives, pitted
- 3 tbsp (45 ml) brown sugar
- pinch saffron
- 1/2 lemon, juiced
- 1 cup (250 ml) slivered almonds, toasted
- 3 cups (750 ml) couscous
- 4 1/2 cups (1125 ml) boiling water

This is a wonderful recipe inspired by North African cuisine. It is a colorful, vegetarian dish with vibrant flavors.

- Wendy Grater

METHOD

1. In the wok, heat the oil and sauté the onion and garlic.
2. Add the sweet potatoes, beans, red peppers, soy chunks, tomatoes and all the spices except for the saffron and cook at a high temperature for 5 minutes, stirring frequently.
3. Add the vegetable stock, prunes, apricots and the liquid from the artichokes.
4. Cover and simmer for 20 minutes or until the vegetables are tender.
5. Stir in the artichokes, olives, brown sugar and saffron. Simmer for another 5 to 10 minutes.
6. While you are waiting, toast the almonds in a dry frying pan.
7. In a separate stainless steel bowl, pour 3 1/2 cups (875 ml) of boiling water over the couscous and let it stand for 5 minutes.
8. Fluff the couscous with a fork.
9. Serve the stew over the couscous and garnish with toasted almonds.

DRESS IT UP!
Make sure you have a few camels standing nearby to add some North African ambience. A moose or caribou will do.

VEGETARIAN LASAGNA

No leftovers, guaranteed! Whenever I make this lasagna, I think of one particular day on the Mountain River in Canada's Northwest Territories. We had made camp after a day of heavy rain. After putting up the tarp and heating up some hot chocolate, I prepared the lasagna in the Dutch oven. As it was cooking, I noticed that the water level of the river had risen so much that it was encroaching on our campsite. We ended up moving up to higher ground, twice, and all the while the lasagna kept on cooking in the Dutch oven. Finally, after a well-earned dinner, we were flooded out of the site for a final time, had to pack up our gear and hit the water in our canoes again at 10:30 at night. I was thankful that we had such a nutritious and warm meal in our stomachs and that we were in the Arctic, where the daylight lasts almost all night!

- Wendy Grater

DRESS IT UP!
Serve with garlic bread and a Caesar salad.

METHOD
1. Heat the briquettes for the Dutch oven or get your oven ready to bake at 350°F (175°C).
2. For the sauce, sauté the onion and garlic in the olive or canola oil.
3. Add the tomatoes and tomato paste.
4. After a few minutes, add the dried broccoli, mushrooms, peppers, herbs and brown sugar.
5. Simmer for a few minutes and add 1/4 cup (60 ml) of water to thin the sauce.
6. Stir in the spices.
7. In a separate bowl, combine the cottage, ricotta, and parmesan cheeses with the egg powder.
8. Grate the mozzarella and cheddar.
9. To assemble the lasagna, start with a quarter of the sauce in the bottom of the Dutch oven.
10. Cover the sauce with four noodles.
11. Spread another quarter of the sauce over the noodles.

Serves 6
75 minutes
Effort Level: III

INGREDIENTS:
- 2 tbsp (30 ml) olive or canola oil
- 2 cloves garlic, crushed
- 1 onion, chopped
- 28 oz can (796 ml) crushed tomatoes, or 2 cups (500 ml) dried and rehydrated
- 7 1/2 oz can (220 ml) tomato paste, or 1/2 cup (125 ml) dried and rehydrated
- 1 cup (250 ml) dried broccoli
- 1 cup (250 ml) dried mushrooms
- 1/2 cup (125 ml) dried green and red peppers
- 2 tsp (10 ml) dried oregano
- 1 tsp (5 ml) dried basil
- 1 tbsp (15 ml) brown sugar
- 18 oz (500 g) low fat cottage cheese
- 18 oz (500 g) low fat ricotta cheese
- 1 cup (250 ml) parmesan cheese, grated
- 1 tbsp (15 ml) egg powder
- 1 zucchini, shredded
- 12 no-cook lasagna noodles
- 18 oz (500 g) mozzarella cheese, grated
- 18 oz (500 g) cheddar cheese, grated
- 1 cup (250 ml) parmesan or romano cheese

12. Spread half of the cheese filling on top of the sauce.
13. Spread a third of the grated cheeses on top of the cheese filling.
14. Repeat steps 11 through 13.
15. Top with a final layer of noodles, sauce and the remaining cheese.
16. Cook in the Dutch oven for 45-60 minutes or until bubbly and smelling delicious!

Tips!

Because the noodles are the no-cook variety, they do not need to be boiled ahead of time. However, to allow the noodles to absorb the moisture they require, your sauce should be soupier than it would be for regular noodles. Add water to the sauce mix if necessary.

TURKEY POT PIE

This is another hearty, tasty meal for hungry bellies.

Serves 12
60 minutes
Effort Level: II

INGREDIENTS:
- 2 tbsp (30 ml) olive oil
- 1 onion, chunked
- 6 potatoes, cubed
- 4 carrots, sliced
- 1 cup (250 ml) dried mushrooms
- 2 cup (500 ml) freeze-dried turkey chunks
- 1 cup (250 ml) soy chunks
- 1 cup (250 ml) freeze-dried peas
- 1 cup (250 ml) freeze-dried corn
- 1 cup (250 ml) freeze-dried green beans
- 1 pkg (110 ml) cream of mushroom soup mix
- 3 cups (750 ml) tea biscuit mix
- 1 tsp (5 ml) thyme
- salt and pepper to taste

METHOD
1. Heat the briquettes for the Dutch oven.
2. In a large pot, heat the oil and sauté onions until translucent.
3. Add potatoes and carrots. Cover with water, bring to a boil and cook for 15 minutes.
4. Add dried mushrooms, turkey, soy chunks, peas, beans and corn.
5. In a separate bowl, mix cream of mushroom soup mix with 1 cup (250 ml) milk, then add to pot and stir well.
6. Pour the stew into a 12-inch (30 cm) Dutch oven.
7. Stir water into the tea biscuit mix until it is a soft and sticky mixture somewhere between batter and dough.
8. Spoon batter over the stew mixture so that it covers the surface and cook in the Dutch oven 20 minutes, or until biscuit topping is golden.

VARIATIONS!

You can also cook this in one pot. Instead of transferring the stew to the Dutch oven, keep it in the large pot and make sure it is very hot. Mix the tea biscuit mix as above and spoon small balls of the dough into the hot stew, one at a time. Allow to cook like dumplings in the stew mix.

DESSERTS

DESSERTS There's always room for dessert. Some of these recipes are fast and simple, others take more time and attention. What you make will depend on the type of day and the type of dinner you've had.

UNBAKED CHOCOLATE DROP COOKIES

Serves 6

5 minutes

Effort Level: I

INGREDIENTS:
- 2 cups (500 ml) sugar
- 1/4 cup (60 ml) butter
- 1/4 cup (60 ml) shortening
- 6 tbsp (90 ml) cocoa
- 3 cups (750 ml) oatmeal
- 1/2 tsp (2 ml) salt
- 1 cup (250 ml) coconut, shredded
- 1 tsp (5 ml) vanilla

This recipe comes from my mom's kitchen. This is a good one if you're not taking an oven.

- Mark Scriver

METHOD
1. Heat the butter, shortening and sugar until it boils and then remove immediately from heat.
2. Stir in the remaining ingredients.
3. Drop the dough by the spoonful onto a plate to cool.

VARIATIONS!
You can reduce the coconut and oatmeal slightly and add slivered almonds and small pieces of candied cherries or citrus peel instead.

You can also use 1/2 cup (125 ml) of butter and omit the shortening. If you choose this option and use salted butter, omit the salt.

CHOCOLATE FONDUE

Chocolate Fondue is an impressive, delicious and easy dessert for anytime during the trip. However, it tastes best with fresh fruit so you might want to serve it on the first or second night before the more delicate fruits like strawberries, cherries, bananas and grapes perish.

If you have it later in the trip, it can work with melons, apples, oranges, canned fruit such as mandarin oranges, dried fruit like apple rings, figs, papaya, pineapple - or even cake or cookies.

Chocolate burns easily so heat it carefully. A foolproof way is to use a double boiler as described below.

METHOD
1. Put the chocolate in a small pot, and put three equal-sized stones in the bottom of a bigger pot.
2. Put water in the bigger pot and bring it to a boil.
3. Place the smaller pot into the bigger pot, then keep the water in the bigger pot just below boiling.
4. Melt the chocolate, then add the cream or milk (which can be made from powdered milk) and the butter.
5. Serve in the small pot.

Serves 6
10 minutes
Effort Level: I

INGREDIENTS:
- 2 cups (500 ml) chocolate chips or other chocolate
- 1/2 cup (125 ml) milk, cream, or splash of liqueur
- 1 tbsp (15 ml) butter
- 1 tsp (5 ml) vanilla
- 1 1/2 cups (375 ml) fruit, cubed

POPCORN

Serves 6

10 minutes

Effort Level: I

INGREDIENTS:
- 1/3 cup (80 ml) canola oil
- 1/2 cup (125 ml) popping corn
- 1/4 cup (60 ml) butter

For a light dessert or a late-night snack, try popcorn. In this era of microwaves and hot air poppers, corn popped in hot oil will be a real treat. As well as a delicious snack, making popcorn is an entertaining and social event with everyone gathered around the stove or fire.

A round-bottomed wok is ideal for making popcorn, but any large pot will work. You'll also need a lid. If your wok doesn't come with one, use a large stainless steel bowl. I use leather gloves to handle the hot wok and have the channel lock pliers or pot grippers nearby as well.

METHOD

1. For one batch heat 2 or 3 tbsp (30-45 ml) of oil. This will require your constant attention. You want a fair bit of heat but not so much that the oil smokes.
2. When the oil is hot, add 2 tbsp (30 ml) of popping corn and put the lid on. When the popcorn starts popping, keep the wok moving so the popcorn doesn't burn. When all the corn has popped, remove it from the heat.
3. Melt the butter and mix it into the popcorn.

Tips!

Keep the batches small and find the right temperature setting on your stove or fire. Be cautious with the hot oil.

VARIATIONS!

Try these combinations: salt, pepper and garlic powder; Tabasco and soy sauce; soy sauce and parmesan cheese; mild or hot curry powder; or cinnamon and brown sugar.

S'MORES

Serves 6
30 minutes
Effort Level: I

INGREDIENTS:
• 10 oz bag (300 g) marshmallows
• 8 oz (220 g) chocolate bar or
  chocolate chips
• 16 oz box (480 g) graham crackers

It is easy to make life more complicated than it needs to be. Here's a camp classic, and a reminder that desserts don't have to be fancy to be delicious: graham crackers, chocolate, marshmallows and a fire. This dessert requires no dishes.

METHOD
1. Toast a marshmallow to golden brown and squish it with some chocolate between two graham crackers. The myth is that the marshmallow will melt the chocolate.

VARIATIONS!
Eat the chocolate while you're toasting the marshmallows and finish off the graham crackers when everything else is gone.

BANANA BOATS

Serves 6
20 minutes
Effort Level: I

INGREDIENTS:
• 6 bananas
• 1/2 pkg (150 g) mini marshmallows
• 12 oz pkg (360 g) chocolate chips,
  peanut butter chips, or both

Banana boats, along with s'mores, are terrific on family trips because kids love them and they can make their own.

METHOD
1. Pull back one strip of the peel from each banana, but don't remove it.
2. Cut a groove like a ditch into the flesh of the banana, lengthwise and eat the fruit that you remove.
3. Line the groove with mini marshmallows, chocolate and peanut butter chips.
4. Replace the strip of peel so that it covers the marshmallows and chips, and then wrap the whole banana in aluminum foil.
5. Place the bananas on the grill over a low fire, or snuggle them into the coals and cook for about 15 minutes.
6. Gently remove them from the heat and remove the tinfoil. Peel back the skin and eat the contents with a spoon.

CAROLYN'S ICE FIELD ICE CREAM

At the confluence of Push-Me-Pull-You Creek and Black Feather Creek on the Mountain River, there is a large ice field or aufeis that forms every season and lasts a little longer into summer than other ice and snow. If you arrive in early July, you'll find it at the end of a long day of portaging and lining canoes. The ice field is situated at the most logical place to camp at the end of that day and to my ear calls out a silent challenge to make ice cream the old fashioned way - an unexpected, memorable treat to enjoy surrounded by breathtaking scenery.

If you know you'll camp somewhere that will have ice available, pack some heavy cream and rock salt and see if you can pull this one off. You need two nesting pots that allow at least 1-2 inches of space between the sides of the small pot and the large pot.

- Carolyn Pullen (first tried on Mountain River, 1990, guiding with Jim Risk)

METHOD

1. In smaller of two nesting pots, mix all the ingredients and cover it with lid.
2. Put the smaller pot into larger pot.
3. Mix the salt with ice and pack it in the space between the two pots, then cover the large pot with its lid.
4. Let it sit for about 10 minutes, then remove the lids and lightly stir the cream mixture.
5. Repeat step 4 until the mixture thickens into ice cream, usually about half an hour.

VARIATIONS!

For chocolate ice cream, add 4 tablespoons (60 ml) cocoa and a pinch of salt to the mix.

Tips!

If the ice cream is not freezing quickly enough, try adding more salt to the snow/ice. If the snow between the pots melts too quickly, add more snow. A delicate art, but well worth the effort!

Serves 6
35 minutes
Effort Level: IV

INGREDIENTS:
- 1 cup (250 ml) heavy cream
- 1 cup (250 ml) light cream
- 1 egg, beaten, or 1 tbsp (15 ml) egg powder with 1 tbsp water
- 1/2 cup (125 ml) sugar
- 1 tsp (5 ml) vanilla extract
- 1 1/2 cups (375 ml) rock or regular salt

FRED'S SPRITE CAKE

Serves 6

45 minutes

Effort Level: II

INGREDIENTS:
- 1 pkg (550 g) white or yellow cake mix
- 14 oz can (398 ml) sliced peaches, drained
- 1 can (335 ml) lemon-lime soft drink

METHOD

1. Heat the briquettes for the Dutch oven or get your oven ready to bake at 350°F (175°C).
2. Pour drained fruit into a greased 10-inch Dutch oven or baking pan.
3. Sprinkle the dry cake mix evenly over fruit.
4. Pour the lemon-lime soft drink evenly over all the cake mix. DO NOT MIX!
5. Cover with foil and bake for 20 minutes.
6. Remove foil and continue baking until the batter has set, usually about 20 minutes.
7. Let cool completely - the cake will become juicier as it cools.

CHEESE PLATE

This is one of our favorite combinations but of course you can assemble any sort of cheese plate for a savory and sweet nibble after dinner.

METHOD Serve on a tray or make individual servings on plates. Only cut the portion of the fruit and cheese that you know will get eaten. You can cut more as you go.

DRESS IT UP!
Serve with port, ice wine, a non-alcoholic sparkling juice, coffee or tea.

Tips!

Don't overdo it, either in terms of quantities or varieties. The focus should be on quality not quantity.

Serves 6

10 minutes

Effort Level: I

INGREDIENTS:
- 9 oz (250 g) blue cheese
- 9 oz (250 g) cheddar cheese
- 9 oz (250 g) feta cheese
- 1 pkg crackers
- 1 honeydew melon
- 1 1/2 cups (375 ml) hazelnuts
- 6 dark chocolate truffles
- Red and green grapes

CAMP CAKE

This is an easy crowd pleaser if you're taking an oven - and haven't we already convinced you that you need to take an oven? This recipe shows you how to adapt a regular cake mix to camp cooking, but if you have a favorite recipe that you make from scratch, pack the ingredients and make that instead.

If someone is celebrating a birthday on the trip, a double-layered frosted cake with candles will make it a really special evening and create a lasting memory.

You need two 8 or 9 inch pans. Before the trip, cut out the directions from the box and recycle the rest, or make note of what needs to be added to the dry ingredients.

METHOD

To make the cake:

1. Heat the briquettes for the Dutch oven or get your oven ready to bake at 350°F (175°C).
2. Substitute egg powder and water for real eggs and otherwise follow the directions on the box.
3. Pour the batter into greased pans. The batter should be about 1 to 2 inches (2 1/2 - 5 cm) deep.
4. Bake for about 30 minutes. Test it by inserting a clean twig - it's done when it comes out without batter stuck to it, or when the top rebounds to a light touch.
5. If you're using frosting, let it cool (if you have the patience). For a single layer cake, you can frost it and serve it straight from the pan. For a double layer cake remove the cake from the pans when they come out of the oven and assemble.

To make the frosting and assemble the cake:

1. Combine the icing sugar, butter, milk and vanilla in a bowl with a spoon, smearing the butter into the icing sugar.
2. To frost a double-layer cake, put one cake top down and the other top up with a layer of fruit, jam or frosting in between

continued on next page...

Short Cut!

Use pre-made frosting, available at the grocery store in vacuum-sealed pouches.

Serves 6
45 minutes
Effort Level: II
Short Cut Option

INGREDIENTS:
- 1 box (550 g) your choice of cake mix
- water, according to box
- milk (from powder), according to box
- oil, according to box
- 1 tbsp (15 ml) each of egg powder and water for every real egg required
- 3/4 cup (175 ml) icing sugar
- 1 1/2 tbsp (25 ml) butter
- 1 tsp (5 ml) milk
- 1/2 tsp (2 ml) vanilla

continued from previous page...

the layers. Dump most of the icing on top of the cake and spread with a knife. Try to spread with as few strokes as possible because the icing will pick up crumbs from the cake. Spread the icing along the side of the cake with one continuous swoop with the knife by turning the plate gently as you do it.

DRESS IT UP!

Add the grated zest from 1/2 of a lemon or orange to the frosting. Top the cake with chocolate chips, crushed nuts or pieces of fruit. A baker friend of mine used to adorn black forest cakes with green olives, but we'll leave decisions like that up to you.

Tips!

Heat the pan or Dutch oven slightly before greasing it to make sure it is completely dry and you'll have fewer problems with the cake sticking.

VARIATIONS!

For spice or carrot cakes, you can make a cream cheese icing. Substitute an equal amount of cream cheese for the butter and milk.

APPLE CRISP

This is a pretty common and easy trip dessert. You can use fresh or dried apples.

Often people add rolled oats or granola to the topping, but in my opinion that can taste too much like breakfast. Without the oats and with lots of sugar it's a gooey and crunchy dessert.

- Mark Scriver

METHOD

1. Heat the briquettes for the Dutch oven or get your oven ready to bake at 350°F (175°C).
2. Rehydrate the apples and drain them, reserving 1/2 cup (125 ml) of the apple water.
3. Place the apples, brown sugar and remaining water in a greased Dutch oven or baking pan.
4. Combine the topping ingredients and sprinkle it over the apples.
5. Bake for 30 minutes.

Serves 6
45 minutes
Effort Level: I

INGREDIENTS:
- 4 cups (1 L) dried apples
- 1/2 cup (125 ml) water
- 2 tbsp (30 ml) brown sugar
- 1/3 cup (80 ml) butter
- 3/4 cup (175 ml) all purpose flour
- 1 cup (250 ml) brown sugar
- 1 tsp (5 ml) cinnamon
- 1/2 tsp (2 ml) nutmeg

DRESS IT UP!

Serve *Carolyn's Ice Field Ice Cream* if you can. Just hop on over to the nearest glacier or aufeis and whip some up.

VARIATIONS!

You can add rolled oats or granola if you must or fruit and nuts like cranberries and almonds. I like to add 1 package of freeze-dried applesauce (rehydrated) to the dried apple mixture for a 'creamier' texture.

A Dutch oven is the easiest way to cook this, but if you don't have an oven, you can use a frying pan with a tight lid. Cook it over a slow fire with a little extra water and you'll get reasonable results.

DUMP CAKE

This is a rather unappetizing title for a delicious and ridiculously simple dessert. It was perhaps strategically named. "You don't want any of this dump cake, do you?"

- Elsie Scriver

Serves 12
40 minutes
Effort Level: I

INGREDIENTS:
- 16 oz can (450 g) sliced peaches
- 1 box (550 g) white cake mix
- 1/2 cup (125 ml) butter, melted
- 1/2 cup (125 ml) coconut

METHOD
1. Heat the briquettes for the Dutch oven or get your oven ready to bake at 350°F (175°C).
2. Pour the peaches in the bottom of a baking pan or Dutch oven. There is no need to grease the pan.
3. Sprinkle the dry contents of the cake mix over the fruit evenly but do not stir.
4. Drizzle the melted butter over the cake mix and sprinkle the coconut on top. It's that simple.
5. Bake for 30 minutes.

Tips!
Try other fruit and other cake mix flavors, like sliced pears with chocolate cake.

BIG CRUNCH SQUARES

This is a great, nutritious twist on the standard Rice Krispie square recipe. I first had this when traveling with a van-full of teenagers, heading for a ski and snowboarding holiday in Quebec. One of the kid's parents had made these to last for the week, but they were gone before we got to the mountain!

- Wendy Grater and Paula Mullen, Parry Sound

METHOD
1. Toast the nuts in a dry frying pan over medium heat. Stir regularly until they are golden.
2. Melt butter or margarine and marshmallows in a large pot or wok, stirring constantly, then remove from heat.
3. Still stirring, immediately add the nuts and seeds to the marshmallow mixture, followed by the dried fruit and half the volume of corn flakes.
4. Add the remaining cornflakes slowly until a stiff consistency is achieved. Press into a greased pan or griddle.
5. Cut into squares and enjoy.

DRESS IT UP!
Drizzle a little melted chocolate over the top in a swirling pattern.

Tips!
As soon as you have pressed the ingredients into the pan, add hot water to the pot and let it soak for 10 - 15 minutes to make the clean-up much easier.

Serves 12
15 minutes
Effort Level: I

INGREDIENTS:
- 7 cups (1.75 L) corn flake cereal
- 1/2 cup (125 ml) butter or margarine
- 18 oz (500 g) marshmallows
- 1/2 cup (125 ml) sunflower seeds
- 3/4 cup (175 ml) sesame seeds
- 1/2 cup (125 ml) pumpkin seeds
- 1/2 cup (125 ml) pecan pieces
- 1/2 cup (125 ml) hazelnut pieces
- 1/2 cup (125 ml) dried apricots, chopped
- 1/2 cup (125 ml) dried cranberries
- 3/4 cup (175 ml) raisins

BAKED GOODS

BAKED GOODS Baked Goods are surprisingly easy
to make in a camp kitchen and are so delicious they are worth every
minute of preparation. Some of these recipes don't even require
an oven.

BANNOCK

Bannock is the traditional camp bread. I've had bannock served by Inuit of Baffin Island, Dene of the Mackenzie Valley and Ojibwa of northern Ontario. Each recipe has been slightly different but had in common that it was delicious, went well with a big mug of tea and inspired excellent storytelling.

Bannock can be baked in a Dutch oven or Outback Oven, fried in a good (preferably cast iron) frying pan, or wrapped on a stick and toasted over an open campfire.

- Wendy Grater

METHOD
1. Mix the flour and baking powder.
2. Cut in the lard, butter or margarine with knives or a fork until it is blended into pea-sized chunks.
3. Add water until the dough can be handled without being sticky.
4. Knead lightly and only until you have a smooth consistency.

FRYING METHOD
1. Heat the oil in a frying pan.
2. Divide the dough into two batches for cooking and sprinkle with flour.
3. Form each loaf into a large, flat disc up to 2 inches (5 cm) thick. A thinner loaf will be easier to cook but not as moist and fluffy as a thicker one.
4. Remove the pan from the heat and pat the dough into it.
5. Return the pan to the heat. Over a low heat, fry the bannock until golden on the first side.
6. Flip it and repeat for the second side. If the bannock is thick, cover the pan with a lid to help the dough cook more evenly.

DRESS IT UP!
Serve with butter, jam or honey, and a pot of tea.

Serves 6
30 minutes
Effort Level: II

INGREDIENTS:
- 2 1/2 cups (625 ml) flour
- 1/4 cup (60 ml) lard, butter or margarine
- 1 tbsp (15 ml) baking powder
- 1 cup (250 ml) water
- 2 tbsp (30 ml) canola oil

Oven Method

1. Heat the briquettes for the Dutch oven or get your oven ready to bake at 350°F (175°C).
2. Grease the Dutch oven or baking pan.
3. Divide the dough and form into flat loaves as described for the frying method above; pat into the pan or Dutch oven and cook for about 15 minutes or until golden.

Campfire Method

1. Roll the dough into a long rope, with a 3/4 inch (1 1/2 cm) diameter.
2. Divide it into ten 8-inch (20 cm) lengths.
3. Wrap a piece of dough in a snug coil around the end of a cooking stick that is about as big around as an adult thumb.
4. Hold the stick over hot coals for 10 minutes or until golden.

Tips!

Make sure that your cooking fire is not burning too hot. It is better to let it cook slowly over a bed of red-hot coals or a low fire, than to rush it and let the bannock get scorched by flames.

VARIATIONS!

Add freshly picked or dried berries to the mix before cooking.

YEAST BREAD

Breads made with baking powder and/or baking soda are tasty, simple and will keep well for a day or two but yeast bread has such a great texture, taste and smell and it is more resilient to crumbling. Yeast bread does take some extra time to rise before it goes in the oven and more attention during the preparation to keep the dough warm but it is very rewarding to make, and it's really delicious.

Because yeast bread takes so much more time, bake it during the evening for the next day or make it on rest days.

METHOD

1. Dissolve 1 tsp of sugar in 1/2 cup of warm water. Sprinkle the dry yeast into the cup and let it stand for 5 minutes. The water should be just warmer than body temperature (105 to 115°F, or 40 to 45°C). Too hot and you'll kill the yeast. The yeast will start to grow and make a frothy foam on top of the water. Yeast, along with the gluten in wheat flour, gives bread its texture.
2. Mix all the remaining ingredients in a large bowl, but use only one cup of the flour. The water you use here should start a bit warmer because it will cool before you add the yeast mixture. Do not omit the salt because it is critical to control the yeast as well as add flavor.
3. Add the yeast and mix thoroughly.
4. Gradually add about 5 or 6 cups of the flour or until the dough becomes too sticky and stiff to stir.
5. Flour your hands and start kneading the dough by firmly but gently gathering and fold the dough over on itself. Let the weight of your upper body do the work as you push with the heels of your hands. Turn the dough constantly to mix and re-distribute all the ingredients in the dough. Do this for about 5 to 10 minutes. As the flour absorbs moisture from the dough, add more flour. You can continue kneading the bread in the bowl but a great place to knead it is on an overturned canoe. Keep your hands and the bowl or canoe lightly floured.

Tips!

Bread baking sounds quite involved and it is a bit of an art but unless you kill the yeast with too much heat during the rising phases, it is also hard to truly go wrong.

On a warm evening when you're not in a rush you can get the dough mixed and kneaded in about 15 minutes and then ignore it while you make supper. (Even in more adverse conditions, where the dough gets cold and doesn't rise much, you will still get a tasty loaf out of it that will still be good at lunch). Knead it again after the meal and it will be ready for the oven by the time people are starting on the dishes. One of the loaves will usually provide lunch for six people. It will be hard to resist eating the other one as it comes out of oven.

Serves 12 (makes 2 round loaves)
2-3 hours
Effort Level: III

INGREDIENTS:
- 2 pkg (14 g) dry active granular yeast
- 3 cups (750 ml) warm water
- 1 tsp (5 ml) sugar
- 2 tbsp (30 ml) egg powder
- 1/4 cup (60 ml) butter
- 1/2 cup (125 ml) milk powder
- 1 1/2 tsp (7 ml) salt
- 1/4 cup (60 ml) sugar
- 9 cups (2 1/4 L) wheat flour

VARIATIONS!

To this basic recipe you can add things like nuts, fruit, grated cheese, onions, spices and molasses. There is more gluten in all-purpose white or bread flour so if you want to use other flours such as rye, corn or rice flour, just use a cup or two for flavor.

6. When it's ready, the surface of the dough will rebound to your touch. A pinch of it will feel a bit like an earlobe.

7. Put the bread back in the bowl it was mixed in and cover it with another bowl.

8. Try to keep it warm so it can rise and double in size, caused by the fermenting of the yeast. This first rising fermentation period can take as little as half an hour if the dough is kept warm and away from drafts, or about an hour or more in cooler conditions. You can set it in a sheltered spot near the fire, but don't let it get too hot or the yeast will die and the bread won't rise. For a temperature reference point, if you were making bread at home, you could simply put it in an oven with just the light turned on for heat.

9. When the dough has approximately doubled in size, punch it down to get rid of the large air bubbles and knead it again for 5 minutes or so. Add flour as required to prevent it from sticking.

10. Cut the dough in half, shape it into two round loaves and place them in two greased pans or Dutch ovens. The bread should be an inch or two from the edge of the pan. Cover.

11. Cover and let the dough rise for 20 minutes or so, while you heat the briquettes for the Dutch oven or get your oven ready to bake at 350°F (175°C).

12. Bake the loaves for 35 to 45 minutes.

CRANBERRY NUT BREAD

Make this loaf at home before you leave and serve it early on in your trip for breakfast. It will be a welcome treat and should stay intact if you pack it carefully.

Makes 2 small loaves

90 minutes

Effort Level: IV

INGREDIENTS:
- 2 cups (500 ml) all purpose flour
- 1 1/2 tsp (7 ml) baking powder
- 1/2 cup (125 ml) sugar
- 1/3 cup (80 ml) butter
- 1 egg, beaten
- 3/4 cup (175 ml) orange juice
- 1 tsp (5 ml) grated orange rind
- 1 cup (250 ml) dried cranberries, chopped
- 1/2 cup (125 ml) pecans, chopped

METHOD
1. Sift flour, baking powder and sugar together in a bowl.
2. Cut in the butter until the mixture looks like coarse meal.
3. In a separate bowl, combine egg with orange juice and rind.
4. Stir the wet ingredients into the dry ingredients until just blended.
5. Fold in the cranberries and nuts and pour into a greased and floured loaf pan(s).
6. Bake at 400°F (200°C) for 10 minutes.
7. Reduce heat to 350°F (175°C) and bake 15-20 minutes longer or until tops are dark brown and a toothpick inserted into the center of a loaf comes out clean.
8. Turn out the loaves when they are still slightly warm and cool on a wire rack.

CORNMEAL SODA BREAD

This is a dense and filling loaf. The cornmeal gives it a
crunchy texture.

Makes 2 small loaves
60 minutes
Effort Level: II

INGREDIENTS:
- 4 cups (1 L) all purpose flour
- 1/2 cup (125 ml) cornmeal
- 1 tbsp (15 ml) baking powder
- 1 1/2 tsp (7 ml) baking soda
- 1/2 cup (125 ml) sunflower seeds
- 1 tsp (5 ml) salt
- 2 tbsp (30 ml) sugar
- 1 cup (250 ml) vegetable oil
- 3 tbsp (45 ml) egg powder
- 1 3/4 cups (425 ml) milk

METHOD

1. Heat the briquettes for the Dutch oven or get your oven
   ready to bake at 350°F (175°C).
2. Combine all ingredients and knead for 2 - 3 minutes until the
   dough has an even consistency.
3. Put in a greased pan or Dutch oven and bake for 35 to
   40 minutes.

LOGAN LOAF

A nutritious and delicious quick bread that is great to fill the hunger cracks on a cold or active day. Slice the bread and serve with plain cream cheese, honey or good old peanut butter and jam.

On one memorable trip on the Nahanni River, I had excitedly told the trip members how much I loved Logan Bread, what a tasty treat it was, how there were few better things to bake on a trip. By day 6, when we were to have it for the first time, the anticipation was high. At breakfast, I mixed up the dough and cooked it in the Dutch oven. The delicious scent of fresh baking wafted through the air, making our mouths water. After 30 minutes of cooking, I opened the lid of the oven, and there it was - not a loaf at all, but a little flat disc! It hadn't risen at all. I guess we (I mean "I") had forgotten to add any of the leavening agents. We ended up having something else for lunch, but we had a rousing game of Logan Loaf frisbee on the gravel bar!

- Wendy Grater, Nahanni 2001

METHOD

1. Heat the briquettes for the Dutch oven or get your oven ready to bake at 350°F (175°C).
2. Combine the dry ingredients and then add walnuts and raisins.
3. Stir in the oil and gradually add the water.
4. Put in a greased pan or Dutch oven and bake for 50-55 minutes.

Serves 12
30 minutes
Effort Level: II

INGREDIENTS:
- 2 cups (500 ml) whole wheat flour
- 2 cups (500 ml) all purpose flour
- 2 cups (500 ml) rye flour
- 2 cups (500 ml) rolled oats
- 1 cup (250 ml) brown sugar
- 4 tsp (20 ml) baking powder
- 2 tsp (10 ml) baking soda
- 6 tbsp (90 ml) egg powder
- 2/3 cup (160 ml) milk powder
- 2 tsp (10 ml) cinnamon
- 1 cup (250 ml) walnuts
- 1 cup (250 ml) raisins
- 1/3 cup (80 ml) oil
- 4 cups (1 L) water

Photo Credits

RICK MATTHEWS: xii, 9, 11, 21, 22, 25, 26, 28, 29, 37, 38, 65, 67, 69, 75, 80, 84, 87, 99, 102, 104, 106, 117, 118, 120, 122, 129, 139, 142, 143, 145, 146, 151, 153, 155, 158, 177, 178, 188, 198

JOCK BRADLEY: v, 5, 6, 12, 20, 27, 34, 41, 43, 48, 55, 57, 66, 76, 86, 88, 92, 96, 111, 115, 116, 127, 150, 163, 168, 186, 202

PAUL VILLECOURT: vii, 10, 16, 30, 50, 59, 62, 72, 83, 89, 134, 149, 169, 174

MAUREEN BRETZ: 47, 56, 57, 135, 137, 157, 201

MARILYN SCRIVER: iii, 18, 61, 112, 132, 170, 193

STEVE MACDONALD: 52, 87, 119, 162, 183, 195

ANGUS MACDONALD: 46, 54, 68, 69, 166

WENDY GRATER: 53, 95, 125, 185

CRAIG RENDER: 66, 165, 172

REBECCA SANDIFORD: 14, 19, 42

PETER WILSON: 107, 191

SHAWN TAYLOR: 23, 36, 70, 180

TINA & BRAD ALFREY: 44, 197

FRED LOOSEMORE: 78

JULIAN GREENWOOD: 40

JANNA SWALES: 35

KEN WHITING: 64

MARCUS WATERREUS: 31

TIM WHEELER: 90

WAYNE & DORIS ALBRECHT: 58

Also Available From
THE **HELICONIA PRESS**

WWW.**HELIPRESS**.COM